Rangers, Rovers and Spindles

Soccer, Immigration and Textiles in New England and New Jersey

Roger Allaway

St. Johann Press

Haworth, NJ

Published in the United States of America
by St. Johann Press
P.O. Box 241
Haworth, N.J. 07641

Library of Congress Cataloging-in-Publication Data

Allaway, Roger.
    Rangers, rovers and spindles : soccer, immigration and textiles in
New England and New Jersey / Roger Allaway.
        p. cm.
    Includes bibliographical references and index.
    ISBN 1-878282-36-0 (alk. paper)
    1. Soccer—New England—History.   2. Soccer—New Jersey—History.
3. Immigrants—Recreation—New England—History.   4. Immigrants—
Recreation—New Jersey–History.   5. Textile workers—Recreation—
New England—History.   6. Textile workers—Recreation—New Jersey
—History.   I. Title.

GV944.N43A44 2005
796.334'0974—dc22

                                                        2005046443

The paper used in this publication meets the minimum
requirements of the American National Standard for
Information Sciences-Permanence of Paper for
Printed Library Materials, ANSI/NISO Z39/48-1992

ISBN 1-878282-36-0

Manufactured in the United States of America

Contents

Foreword

WHEN AMERICAN COLLEGE FOOTBALLERS turned from soccer to rugby in the 1870s, soccer in America was abandoned to the attention of groups of workers, largely immigrants, in several urban areas, who kept it alive for many decades while mainstream America was concentrating on other sports. Perhaps the two most significant of those areas were the West Hudson section of New Jersey, centering on Kearny and Harrison, and southeastern New England, centering on Fall River, Mass.; New Bedford, Mass., and Pawtucket, R.I. In those two regions, the early history of the sport followed strikingly parallel lines. In both, the reasons why soccer flourished there from about 1880 onward had much to do with the presence of substantial immigrant populations attracted by large concentrations of textile mills.

This book tells the story of soccer in those two areas over the decades against that industrial and social background, particularly in the sport's heyday there, from the era of 19th-century teams like Kearny Rangers and Fall River Rovers to that of World War II era powers like Kearny Scots and Fall River Ponta Delgada. Both areas faded as major soccer centers with the gradual departure of the textile industry between 1920 and 1950, but the events that once took place there were a significant part of the foundation for everything that has happened in the sport in America in more recent years.

This account of those events makes a significant addition to the growing body of literature on the history of soccer on this side of the Atlantic.

—Colin Jose

Acknowledgments

I HAVE HAD THIS BOOK IN MIND for a number of years, ever since I first was struck by the parallels between the way that soccer took root in Kearny, N.J., and Fall River, Mass., two of its first American outposts. I have felt that other writings on the early development of soccer in the United States gave little time to the non-soccer aspects, to the economic and social background in which early teams in locations like Fall River and Kearny existed.

The first people who began pointing me in the right direction toward learning more about those aspects myself were two college professors, Michael Flamm of Ohio Wesleyan University in Delaware, Ohio, and Gerald Gems of North Central College in Naperville, Ill. Of the many books they led me toward on the American textile industry and immigration to the United States, two stand out. They are *Run of the Mill* by Steve Dunwell and *British Immigrants in Industrial America* by Rowland Berthoff.

Someone who has been especially helpful to me, both through his writings and his direct advice, has been Philip Silvia, a professor of history at Bridgewater State University in Massachusetts, not far from Fall River. Both his doctoral dissertation on labor, politics and religion in Fall River and his *Victorian Vistas* books about Fall River have been invaluable, and he has been helpful to me in a number of other ways.

Another person who has been equally helpful has been Colin Jose, the historian of the National Soccer Hall of Fame, who was my co-author on two previous books. Colin, who has been interested in Fall River's soccer history much longer than I have, lent me a large amount of materials on Fall River that he has collected over the years and helped me to find many useful items in the archives of the Hall of Fame. Further, as I wrote this book, I made frequent use of the game-by-game records that he has painstakingly compiled for his many books.

Both Philip Silva and Colin Jose are among the people who read the manuscript of this book shortly after I completed it. The others are Emmet Linn and Don McKee, both colleagues of mine at the *Philadelphia Inquirer,* and Frank Santamassino, a native of Kearny and former youth soccer player there, who now is an English teacher at Harrison High School.

I have relied heavily on the archives of the National Soccer Hall of Fame, particularly collections of scrapbooks and other memorabilia donated to the Hall of Fame by Louie Souza of Fall River, Sam T.N. Foulds of Salem, N.H., and Milt Miller of New York. In addition to Colin Jose, I have been helped in that effort by Jack Huckel, the Hall of Fame's director of communications.

People who have helped me in various other ways have included David Litterer, without whose research work the Spalding Guides would still be hidden from view; Dan Morrison, whose web site on the Bethlehem Steel team includes a number of newspaper articles that I have quoted; Ken Forbes, a geneology researcher on the West Hudson area whose web site and advice helped me to get started on the history of that area; Patricia Redfearn, reference librarian at the Fall River Public Library; Charlie Waller and George Rogers, leaders of the Kearny Old-timers Soccer Association; Paul Cyr, curator at the New Bedford Public Library; Susan Millard and Paul Martin, reference librarians at the Pawtucket Public Library; Jeanne Zavada, education coordinator at the Slater Mill Historic Site in Pawtucket, Ruth Caswell of Spinner Publications in New Bedford, and numerous reference librarians at the New Jersey State Library in Trenton.

INTRODUCTION:

Where, When and Why

T ACKED TO THE WALL of a cubicle in an office in Philadelphia are two rather similar photographs, taken a few months apart and a few states apart in 2001. Each has a large open expanse in the foreground, one a parking lot in East Newark, N.J., and the other a grassy field in North Tiverton, R.I. In the background of each, most crucially, is a five-story building, one brick and one granite. Both buildings are abandoned textile mills, and they are what tie this story together.

The parking lot in East Newark is the land that once was Clark Field, where the United States played Canada in soccer in 1885, the United States' first international game, and where in that same year the first American Football Association Cup final, in a sense the first national championship game, was played. The brick building in the background once was the Mile End Spool Cotton Mill, part of the Clark Thread Company complex in what, in 1885, still was a part of the town of Kearny, N.J.

The grassy field in North Tiverton is the land that once was Mark's Stadium, where the Fall River Marksmen of the original American Soccer League played their home games in the 1920s, playing just across the state line from Fall River, Mass., in order to be able to charge admission on Sundays, something the Massachusetts blue laws prohibited. The granite building in the background once was the Bourne Mill, one of more than 100 textile mills in and around Fall River, which for a time was the nation's dominant textile center.

Why were both soccer fields located so close to textile mills? Because the textile industry and the immigration that it attracted, particularly from England and Scotland, also brought the sport, which flourished in the areas of Fall River and Kearny as it did in only one other place in the country, the famous soccer hotbed of St. Louis, Mo.

Textiles, immigration and soccer are what this story is about.

THE KEARNY AREA is commonly referred to as West Hudson, meaning the portion of Hudson County west of the Hackensack River. This area includes the present-day towns of Kearny, Harrison and East Newark. There also was a pocket significant to the early history of American soccer about 15 miles to the north in the silk-making city of Paterson, N.J.

The area of southeastern New England in question is less specific. It centers basically on the cities of Fall River and New Bedford, Mass., and Pawtucket, R.I., spanning a distance of about 40 miles, but it also includes the area in between those cities and to a lesser degree some other nearby cities, such as Providence, R.I.

These two areas, hundreds of miles apart, are not normally considered to have much in common with each other, but they are linked here because their histories, at least in soccer terms, are extraordinarily similar. And perhaps a century ago, when teams from those two areas were regularly vying with each other for "national" soccer honors, they were linked with each other in the public mind more than they are today. (Those honors were national in name only, because national soccer organizations in those days really covered only a small portion of the country.)

In both of these places, soccer was *the* sport, drawing respect that it didn't elsewhere. Indeed, it may still be *the* sport in Kearny, which has retained a fair amount of the ethnic flavor that once dominated it. The names Fall River and Kearny don't mean much to most American soccer players of today, but to players in the middle of the 20th century and earlier, both were hallowed names.

In the early years of American soccer, teams from these two areas dominated intersectional soccer competition in the United

States. The main such competition, the American Football Association Cup, was regularly won by New Jersey teams, such as ONT of Kearny, West Hudson of Harrison and True Blues of Paterson; and New England teams, such as Fall River Rovers, Fall River East Ends and Pawtucket Free Wanderers. This strength didn't end there. Fall River Marksmen, New Bedford Whalers and J&P Coats of Pawtucket were among the leading teams of the original American Soccer League in the 1920s, and Ponta Delgada of Fall River, playing on that same field across the state line in Rhode Island, was one of the best American teams of the 1940s. Kearny Scots and Kearny Irish were mainstays of the second American Soccer League up until the 1950s, and Kearny Scots still exist today as an amateur team.

The first supposedly national soccer organization in the United States, the American Football Association, was formed in 1884, at a meeting at a Clark Thread Company building in Newark, N.J.[1] The first soccer team in Fall River, the East Ends, had been formed in 1880,[2] and when the American Football Association held its first cup competition in the 1884–85 season, the 13 entries included two from Fall River.

That American soccer, which may have had its beginnings as far back as the 1860s, experienced such significant early growth in these two places was no accident.

The Clark Thread Company of Paisley, Scotland, decided in the 1860s to move a portion of its manufacturing operations to a location closer to the many Americans among its customers, and chose Newark as that location.[3] The thread-making operation in Newark quickly spread across the Passaic River to Kearny, particularly the portion of Kearny that in 1895 was to separate off as the borough of East Newark. The Clark Thread operations, plus the presence of a linoleum plant that also was the American branch of a Scottish corporation, brought heavy immigration from Scotland to Kearny,[4] and with that immigration came association football, which was never called soccer until students at Oxford University in England gave it that name (along with "rugger" for rugby) in the 1880s.

A similar pattern developed in Fall River. The American textile industry had its beginnings in the 1790s in Pawtucket, and by the early 20th century, New Bedford equalled Fall River as a textile center. In the late 19th century, however, Fall River was the undisputed king, with the local textile industry centering on the production of cotton print cloth.[5] The boom in the textile industry in Fall River had really taken off in the 1870s, and had produced a flood of immigration from the Lancashire region of England,[6] which in addition to being the heart of the English textile industry also was the area of England in which association football had most taken root among working-class people in those same years. In Fall River, as in Kearny, textiles brought immigration and immigration brought football.

IN TALKING ABOUT IMMIGRATION and sports, it is easy to fall into misleading stereotypes. In examining the history of West Hudson, southeastern New England, textiles, immigration and soccer, it is well to remember these pitfalls. Many immigrant groups brought sports traditions with them from their homelands, but not all did, and some brought traditions different from what might be expected in a sterotyped view of them, the sort of view in which soccer is seen as a "foreign sport" in which all immigrants are supposed to be interested. Americans have often applied blanket sterotypes in dealing with immigrants and sports, such as the practice years ago in major-league baseball stadiums in which organists seemed to play "The Mexican Hat Dance" whenever a Latin player came to bat, whether he was Venezuelan, Cuban, Puerto Rican or, on rare occasions, Mexican.

It is especially important to remember in what years a particular group of immigrants came to America. Soccer didn't spread from the English upper classes into the British working classes until the 1870s, and into other countries on the continent of Europe and in South America until the 1880s.[7] If a particular group of immigrants came to America before soccer reached the places they came from, then they couldn't have brought soccer with them to America. This may seem so obvious as to be not worth mentioning, but it is easy to forget. Many Americans today think of soccer as a generalized European thing, and overlook the fact that this was not always so. By the 1880s, when soccer in Kearny and Fall River began, it was popular only in a few small areas of Europe.

Soccer, derived from barely organized mob games played throughout England and elsewhere for centuries, really developed into an organized sport in the middle of the 19th century in the English schools and universities.[8]

Major codifying of the rules took place at Cambridge University in 1848 and in London in 1863. Up to this point, this organized version of the game was restricted to the upper classes who attended those schools and universities, but by the 1870s, it had begun to move into the working classes, particularly in the Lancashire region of northwestern England and the River Clyde valley in Scotland.

Not all immigrant groups brought soccer to America, but those who most heavily did do so included English textile workers emigrating to Fall River in the last decades of the 19th century and Scottish textile and linoleum workers coming to Kearny in the same era. Why did immigrant textile workers arriving in Fall River and Kearny bring soccer with them, while, for example, immigrant packing-house workers arriving in Chicago or immigrant construction workers arriving in New York in the same years did not bring the sport with them? The reason is simple. It was because the first places in which soccer spread into the working classes were the same areas, Lancashire and the valley of the Clyde, that most of those textile workers came from. Those connections are crucially important, worth emphasizing and repeating.

It was a little bit different with the large Portuguese-speaking community of southeastern New England. By the middle of the 20th century, Portugal had become one of Europe's leading soccer powers and southeastern New England had become more identified with the Portuguese than with any other immigrant group. But the Portuguese-speaking immigrants for whom southeastern New England was a prime destination in the late 19th century didn't bring soccer with them to America. The sport didn't reach Portugal until the 1890s and the Azores, which is where most of those immigrants came from, until even later.

Portuguese immigration to New England reached its peak in the second decade of the 20th century.[9] By that time, soccer had reached the Azores. But still, a great many Portuguese-speaking immigrants weren't introduced to soccer until after their trip across the ocean, and Portuguese soccer in New England remained basically amateur, a rung or two below the professional and semipro American Soccer League, for many decades. By the middle of the 20th century, the top levels of American soccer were dotted with Portuguese names like Souza, Braga and Ferreira, but a review of the records of the original American Soccer League, which lasted from 1921 to 1931, will show only a few Portuguese names among the more than 1,000 players.[10] This scarcity may be a factor to some degree of ethnic discrimination, but it also reflects the fact that Portuguese soccer in New England remained amateur, and relatively low-profile, well into the 20th century.

That American Soccer League of 1921–31 was heavily fueled by Scottish immigrants. Scottish immigration to the United States surged in the 1920s, particularly as a result of changes in the immigration laws that favored British immigrants over immigrants from southern Europe.[11] The majority of the spectators may still have been English, but they were joined in the 1920s by thousands of Scotsmen, cheering on their compatriots, who were dominating the teams by then.

Not all immigrants arriving in the United States brought soccer traditions with them. However, a great many of those in Fall River and Kearny by the early 1900s did, and the reasons for that were connected to both *where* they had come from and *when* they had come.

I

Getting Ready
to Play

B Y THE TIME that soccer, or association football, began arriving in the areas of northern New Jersey and southeastern New England where it was to become a passion, many events had taken place, both in the organization of municipalities and the creation of industries, that made those areas fertile ground for the growth of the sport.

The West Hudson area occupies part of a region of marshlands now known as the Meadowlands or the New Jersey Meadows, along with some drier land alongside the marshes. Much of those marshlands today are occupied by landfills and industrial sites, and criss-crossed by major highways and railroad lines, but parts of the meadows, acres of tall marsh grass, are still there, and indicate what the rest must once have looked like. Four hundred years ago, the area was all marsh grass, mile after mile of it, and must have been a stunning sight to the first European explorers who, with their ship anchored in the Hudson River, climbed the hill that now is Jersey City and looked out across this magnificent expanse. (Today, the most interesting view is in the other direction, to the east from Kearny, with the skycrapers of New York projecting above that same hill.)

WEST HUDSON is a sort of a peninsula, although what surrounds it

1

on three sides and makes it a peninsula is not open water but southward flowing rivers, the Hackensack River on the east and the
Passaic River on the west and south. The first major commercial
activity in the area came in the early 1700s, particularly as a result
of the discovery of copper in 1719[1] in the northwestern part of the
peninsula, the area later known as North Arlington. While most of
the peninsula, particularly on its eastern side, is marshlands, there
is a ridge of much higher, more solid land running down the western side of the peninsula, along the Passaic River. All of the area is
rock laid down eons ago as sediment, but the marshland is softer
rock that was eroded more deeply than the ridge.[2] Settlers gradually moved into this ridge, much more habitable than the marshlands
and mostly used for farming and copper mining before the coming
of the textile mills. From there, they expanded into the bottomlands
at the southern tip of the peninsula, the area now occupied by the
town of Harrison. Much of the commercial activity in the area, particularly the thread and linoleum mills, was to take place along the
ridge and in the bottomland, but the southern tip of the marshland
was the scene of some important commercial ventures in the 20th
century, most notably a shipyard that played a crucial role in two
world wars. For the most part, however, the marshland, which
occupies about two-thirds of West Hudson, was unused in those
early years. Perhaps its heaviest "commercial" activity was as a
haven for New York Harbor's river pirates, eventually driven out
in the early 1800s.[3]

The first name given by Europeans, around 1700, to this "peninsula," which the Hackensack indians had called Meghgecticock,
was New Barbadoes. It later went by a series of informal names,
New Barbadoes Neck, Barbadoes Neck, Barbery Neck, Barber's
Neck, Petersborough and Kennedy's Farm, until, in 1815, the residents formally voted to adopt the name of Lodi, after a town in
northern Italy that had figured in the Napoleanic wars.[4]

At this time, Lodi Township was part of Bergen County, but in
later years, it was one of a group of municipalities that petitioned for
a new county to be created out of the southern part of Bergen
County. In 1840, this was done, and a part of Lodi Township became
Harrison Township in the new Hudson County. Harrison Township,
named for the military hero (but not quite yet president) William
Henry Harrison, encompassed the present-day towns of Kearny,

Harrison and East Newark, but in 1840, it all was Harrison. The next division took place in 1867, when all but the southern tip of the township managed to secede from Harrison, and became the township of Kearney, named for Gen. Phillip Kearney, a resident of the area who had been killed in a Civil War battle in Virginia a few years before.

The general's name, and the original name of the township, really was spelled Kearney, not Kearny. The second "e" in the name was somehow omitted—no one seems to know why—at the time of the area's incorporation in 1898. (For convenience, this book will refer to it as Kearny throughout, regardless of the year.) And why did this 1867 secession of Kearny from Harrison take place at all? Here, too, there is uncertainty. Among the reasons cited are concerns over which part of Harrison Township was to pay for road improvements, disputes between farming interests in the northern part of the township and manufacturing interests in the southern part, disagreement over the purchase of railroad company bonds by the township, and simple political disputes between Republicans in the part that became Kearny and Democrats in the part that remained Harrison. All of them may have played a part.

The last major division in forming the political landscape in this area took place in 1895, after the growth of soccer there was well underway. By this time, a large part of the Clark Thread complex had been built in the southern part of Kearny, along the border with Harrison. Because such a large part of Kearny's tax base was located in this small area, it decided to secede, and in 1895 became the borough of East Newark. The name was not a new one. Much of the area, larger than the one-square mile extent of the new borough, had long been referred to as East Newark.[5] This change has caused complications for soccer historians. Many people not familiar with the area have thought that East Newark was a part of Newark, the vastly larger city on the other side of the Passaic River, and events in East Newark have often been referred to as having taken place in Newark.

IN NEARBY PATERSON, about 15 miles north of the West Hudson area, the sequence of events that produced an urban area of similar size in which soccer would flourish were less haphazard.

In 1791, the state of New Jersey founded the Society for the

Establishment of Useful Manufactures, with the objective of creating a center of manufacturing close to the huge market of New York City. The following year, the society selected for its undertaking the location that was to become Paterson. The choice of a location was an obvious one, as it included what was by far the most important element necessary for the manufacturing operations of the day, waterpower. The Great Falls of the Passaic River, dropping about 70 feet, provided tremendous capacity for the turning of waterwheels to generate the power needed to operate machinery in factories. The choice of a name was less obvious. Paterson, after William Paterson, then the governor of New Jersey, was chosen over Hamilton, after Alexander Hamilton, one of the Founding Fathers of the United States and the man who had earlier been the first well-known person to extoll the Great Falls of the Passaic as a potential manufacturing site.

A large part of the hopes of New Jersey in establishing Paterson had to do with cotton, but the making of cotton cloth never really took off there. New England manufacturers got a slight head start in that business and came to dominate it. Paterson turned instead to other products, particularly locomotives for the growing railroads. Then, in 1838, the silk industry was introduced on a tentative basis, and Paterson's future was sealed. By the start of the 20th century, Paterson was firmly established as "The Silk City."

Through all of this, the political boundries and name of Paterson remained largely unchanged. Unlike the towns of the West Hudson area, Paterson didn't evolve. It had been founded whole by the Society for the Establishment of Useful Manufactures.

AT THE SAME TIME that these events were changing the map of northern New Jersey, similar developments were taking place in Pawtucket, Fall River and New Bedford, the three centers of southeastern New England's soccer boom of the late 1800s and early 1900s. In two of them, actually, those developments took place at the same time. In 1862, a compromise between the states of Massachusetts and Rhode Island altered the boundary lines in both Pawtucket and Fall River, even though those cities are about 25 miles apart.

Fall River occupies a fairly steep slope on the east side of Mount Hope Bay, which is an arm of the much larger Narragansett Bay. That slope, thanks to the water that runs down it, gave the place its name. Most of that water is the Quequechan River, a rather short stream that flows out of two small lakes, North Watuppa Pond and South Watuppa Pond, at the top of the slope. (Much of the river has since been buried under development, including an Interstate highway.) The Quequechan, falling more than 130 feet in its two miles,[6] provided enough waterpower to attract the fledgling textile industry to Fall River in the first half of the 19th century. Still, it was not large, barely deserving the name "river," and really had little to do with the runaway growth of that industry in the second half, except for being the reason why so many mills were already there. By the time of that growth, Fall River's textile mills were powered by steam.

Fall River Dreams, a 1994 book that is largely about high school basketball and was written by Providence sportswriter Bill Reynolds, included a vivid description of Fall River, with the way it looks today evoking the way that it once did. Said Reynolds: "It is best viewed at twilight, with the lights twinkling and the large foreboding gray stone mills in shadows. It is almost picturesque then, especially from a distance, with the church spires rising out of the horizon and the city spreading out over the small hills. It is possible then to see it as it once was seventy years ago, back when Fall River was the leading textile city in the world, with 140 mills operating twenty-four hours a day, and the mill owners lived on top of the hill with a view of both the mills and the world they had created. From a distance you don't see the decay, the remnants of a city in decline since after World War I. . . . there is no better symbol of the city's decline than the huge abandoned gray mills, some as long as a city block. They are everywhere."[7]

Three centuries ago, however, Fall River's years of both boom and bust were far in the future. In the 1700s, the area that was to become Fall River was a part of Freetown, a municipality that still exists immediately to the north. In 1803, it was separated from Freetown and given the name of Fallriver. A year after that, the name was changed to Troy, in a rather strange homage to the city of Troy, N.Y. In 1834, the name was changed back to Fall River, this time with the spelling that has remained.[8]

There was one major change yet to come. From 1834 to 1862, there were two Fall Rivers. The city straddled the state line, and there was a Fall River, Mass., north of the line and a Fall River, R.I., south of it. In 1862, as a result of a settlement of a dispute between the two states that had gone all the way to the United States Supreme Court, the state line in Fall River was moved several miles south, bringing both Fall Rivers within Massachusetts. At the same time, in Pawtucket, which also straddled the line, the line was moved several miles east, bringing both Pawtuckets within Rhode Island.[9]

In Pawtucket, the processes that led up to 1862 were similar to those in Fall River. Pawtucket today looks like a fairly logically situated place, although it helps to ignore the tangle of streets, of a sort that is often found in New England cities. Mostly importantly, it has a river tumbling down the center. The city is built on both sides of the river, and it is easy to realize that the river is the reason why the city is there in the first place. It took a while to become one city, however.

Before 1862, that river, the Blackstone, was the state line. On the west side, the Rhode Island side, the village of Pawtucket was a part of the town of North Providence, R.I., as it had been for nearly 100 years. To the east, in Massachusetts, there had been some changes along the way. Until 1812, the area on the east side of the Blackstone River was part of the town of Rehoboth, Mass. The western part of Rehoboth, near the river, was devoted to manfacturing, making use of the waterpower that the falls of the Blackstone provided. The eastern part of the town was farmland, and in 1812, the two were divided, with the eastern section retaining the name of Rehoboth and the section along the river taking the name of Seekonk. A further division took place in 1828. The falls were in the northern, upstream, end of Seekonk, while at the southern end, the river widened and became more placid and there was less waterpower to be had. In 1828, that northern end, where most of the factories were located, was separated off from Seekonk, taking the name of Pawtucket, Mass.[10]

From 1828 to 1862, Pawtucket, Mass., and Pawtucket, R.I., remained on opposite sides of the state line, but with significant social and economic ties to each other. Then, in 1862, at the same time that Fall River, R.I., was made a part of Massachusetts, Pawtucket, Mass., was made a part of Rhode Island. Even after the movement of the state line, however, it was another 12 years before the two parts of Pawtucket were legally merged into a single municipality, and not until 1885 were they incorporated as a city.[11]

In contrast to the hills of Fall River and Pawtucket, New Bedford is located on relatively flat land, at least for the New England coast. The Acushnet River, as it passes New Bedford and is about to enter Buzzards Bay, is a stately flow rather than a torrent. The city slopes gently down toward the waterfront. There is no obvious waterpower here, and it was to New Bedford's fortune (temporarily) that by the time the whaling business faded, steam had begun to become the main source of power for the textile industry.

Although New Bedford was slower than either Fall River or Pawtucket to get into the textile business, being primarily occupied with whaling up until the 1870s, it came into being as a municipality before those two.

The town of Dartmouth was organized in 1664. In 1787, Dartmouth was divided into several parts, one of which was the Bedford Village section of the town, which had become the town's business center. It took the name New Bedford at that time, but did not incorporate as a city under that name until 1847, by which time it was at the height of its reign as the whaling capital of the world.[12]

In this same period, New Bedford, unlike most of Puritan New England, was coming under considerable Quaker influence, particularly through several men who provided much of the early financing for the whaling industry. One result of this Quaker influence was that New Bedford was to enjoy a reputation for racial tolerance for years, and this was to have a large effect on the makeup of its immigrant population. In addition to being particularly receptive to abolitionists in the pre-Civil War years, it also was more receptive than Fall River in later years to Portuguese-speaking black immigrants from the Cape Verde islands.

WEST HUDSON and southeastern New England were, by the last quarter of the 19th century, good places for the arrival of soccer, places where it could flourish. The events that led to that situation had begun in the 1790s, with the first stirrings of the textile industry in the United States. But while soccer did arrive in Fall River and Kearny around 1880 and did flourish there, neither Fall River nor Kearny can be called the birthplace of American soccer.

Fall River and Kearny, along with a few other places, particularly St. Louis, were where soccer first took root among working-class people in America and where it grew, instead of blossoming briefly and then dying out. As had happened in England, American soccer began in the upper classes but didn't really grow until it worked its way into the factory towns, shipyards and other working-class locations. Those places have much more connection to American soccer of today than do sites of earlier events. But those earlier events do take precedence as the birth of soccer on this side of the Atlantic, although the exact when and where of that birth is a matter of dispute that probably will never be settled.

That birthplace may have been Boston. If it was not Boston, then it surely was New Brunswick, N.J. The reason for the uncertainty is that it has never been clear whether the game being played by a group of schoolboys on the Boston Common in the 1860s was soccer or not.

The game that these Boston schoolboys, known as the Oneida Football Club, were playing could have been soccer, rugby or some sort of hybrid. Some people take the idea that the Oneidas were playing soccer and that this was the birth of the sport in the United States almost as an article of faith. Advocates on the other side make the point that the Oneidas began playing in 1862, a year before the meetings in London at which the rules of association football were formulated, and there thus was not yet any such thing as association football.

However, the meetings in 1863 at the Freemasons' Tavern in London were designed to iron out differences among similar games that had existed for several decades, not to invent a new game. At least one of the Oneidas, and perhaps more, had been to England, and might have brought back the rules of one of those games (the Cambridge University rules were first formulated in 1848). So, it is possible that the game that the Oneidas were playing in Boston in the 1860s was an early form of what was to become soccer. Of course, it also is possible that it was not, that this is not what happened. We don't know.

Because of this uncertainty, the first game in the United States that clearly was soccer was not one played by the Oneidas, but rather the famous game between Rutgers and Princeton in New Brunswick in 1869. That game is famous because it has long been called the first game of American football, which it was not. Granted, there were major differences from today's soccer. There were 25 men on a side, the teams changed ends after each goal and the first team to score six goals was the winner.

Regardless of whether the first game of soccer in the United States was played in Boston in 1862 or in New Brunswick in 1869, the light that it lit did not flicker for long. The Oneidas played for only a few years before going on to other things, including Harvard University, which, perhaps significantly, was a leader on the rugby side of the equation when the showdown among football-playing American colleges occured in the mid-1870s. Rutgers and Princeton continued to play soccer for a few more years, but by the late 1870s, they and other colleges had followed Harvard's lead to rugby, which eventually evolved into American gridiron football.

In 1863, when English football-playing schools, colleges and clubs met to iron out the rules, the majority opted for the dribbling game (association football) and rugby football was left to go its own way. In 1876, when American football-playing colleges had their showdown over what set of rules to play by, the majority opted for the handling game (rugby football) and association football was left to go its own way.

WHERE ASSOCIATION FOOTBALL went was particularly to West Hudson and southeastern New England, places where there were large populations of immigrant textile workers. Although West Hudson is a slightly different case, the reason why these immigrants were in southeastern New England is dictated largely by those events of the 1790s in which the American textile industry was spawned.

Those events took place particularly in Pawtucket and revolved very strongly around one man, Samuel Slater.

Samuel Slater is one of the legendary figures of American history, although not as well known as some of his politically minded contemporaries. The most exalted title that has been put around his neck is Father of the American Industrial Revolution. The legend that has been built up around Slater in the last 200 years is that he was a ordinary English mill worker who founded the American textile industry by memorizing the details of cotton spinning machinery, whose exportation was illegal, slipping away to America with the plans in his head, and then reconstructing the machinery from memory. The historians at the Slater Mill Historic Site in Pawtucket, the official keepers of the flame where Slater is concerned, do not dispute Slater's legendary status. What they take issue with is many of the details in that legend, particularly the notion that he did what he did singlehandedly and the idea that the construction in America of cotton spinning machinery was Slater's most significant accomplishment. They feel that what was more important was how, in subsequent years, he organized the methods of operating cotton mills so as to make the industry a financial success. The implication is that there are other people who might eventually have done what Slater did as far as building the machinery, but none who could have matched him as a businessman.

Slater was born in the town of Belper, Derbyshire, England, in 1768, not far from where Richard Arkwright, the inventor of much of the first cotton manufacturing equipment, and Jedediah Strutt opened the world's first successful cotton mill in 1771. By the time he was 14, Slater was apprenticed to Strutt, who was no longer partnered with Arkwright. At this time, and for years afterward, British law forbade the exportation of textile machinery or the departure from British shores of people with knowledge of its operation. In 1789, Slater determined to depart, not because he was an impoverished laborer seeking to better himself (he actually had a substantial inheritance), but because he felt the future of the English textile industry was too limited.

The definitive account of Slater's accomplishments, written for the Slater Mill Historic Site by historian Paul T. Rivard, emphasizes that Slater's reasons for leaving England had to do with his fears for the future of the English textile industry, rather than any immediate personal poverty. Specifically, he was afraid that the industry was overextending itself, and could collapse as a result. Particularly fueling these fears was the fact that Richard Arkwright's patents on the textile manufacturing machinery, which had helped to put a lid on expansion, were overturned in 1785 and the industry was opened to anyone with the capital to get started. In short, Slater set off across the ocean feeling that the future of the textile industry was over the horizon, not behind him.[13]

Slater didn't tell his family that he was leaving, and dressed as a farm laborer to board ship, but his passage to America was not really all that furtive. Penalties for persons with textile knowledge like Slater trying to leave Britain were severe (although nowhere near as draconian as the death by torture that China once decreed for persons giving secrets about silk production to foreigners), but the laws were not difficult to side-step. Slater didn't have to hold his breath all the way across the Atlantic.

The legend, or at least the foreshortened high-school textbook version of it, would have you believe that when Slater reached America, he hit the ground running at putting together the machinery that he had memorized. Actually he remained in New York for a few months before making contact with Moses Brown of Rhode Island, a partner in the firm of Almy and Brown, which was making some feeble attempts in Pawtucket to construct spinning machines. That contact is part of the reason why the American textile industry had its beginning in southeastern New England, and why things that included soccer followed it there, rather than someplace else.

Slater did not wave a magic wand of memory over Almy and Brown's rudimentary spinning machinery and turn it, all by himself, into a replica of Arkwright's, Rivard says. Slater had help from American mechanics, and there were fits and start in the process. Slater had been in Pawtucket less than 10 weeks when he and the Americans succeeded in completing a spinning machine capable of doing the job, but they did so through hard work and experimentation, not through any singleminded feat of memory by the Englishman. A group of American mechanics who had worked on the earlier, unsuccessful, machines, continued to be employed by Almy and Brown and worked as a team with Slater.[14]

Slater and the others had to work even harder to perfect the machines that performed the earlier operations in the cotton manufacturing process, carding, drawing and roving, that prepared the raw cotton for being turned into yarn on the spinning machine.

"The establishment of a successful spinning mill in Pawtucket," says Rivard, "was due to a fortunate convergence of factors: The iron and woodworking skills of the Pawtucket area, the experiments undertaken in the Pawtucket Falls area during 1788 and 1789, and finally Samuel Slater's arrival with his great knowledge of the entire operation of cotton textile machinery."[15] Slater was only the final piece, not the entire puzzle.

Slater's efforts in following years probably were even more important. Pawtucket historian Susan Marie Boucher says, "Contrary to popular belief, his greatest contribution was not in his machine-building ability; rather, it was in his ability to manage the textile business."[16] Boucher points out that Slater believed that the secret of success was to operate the machinery at its fullest capacity, producing as much yarn as possible, whereas Almy and Brown favored an approach that produced goods only for the orders they received.

Rivard fully agrees concerning the significance of Slater's ability to manage the textile business. He notes that during Slater's apprenticeship to Jedediah Strutt, he had learned the principles of sound industrial management, and then applied those principles in Pawtucket. Nevertheless, Slater was frustrated by Almy and Brown's more conservative approach, and was unable to put his own methods fully into operation until he established his own mill in 1797.

This "White Mill" was built on the eastern side of the Blackstone, directly across from the "Old Slater Mill" built four years before. Here, says Rivard, Slater was able to employ his philosophy of manufacturing without interference from his partners and proved that a much larger operation than the 1793 mill was workable. The real impact of the textile industry in Pawtucket dates from 1798, when the White Mill was placed in operation. After that date, the development of cotton mills was much accelerated.

"The American textile industry was certainly launched in Pawtucket," Rivard says, "and Samuel Slater was the central figure in this development. But the industry was not launched when the technology of textile manufacture was transplanted to America. Instead, it was launched when the principles of management learned in Derbyshire [by Slater] were themselves transplanted to Pawtucket. And this, above all else, was Samuel Slater's genius."[17]

So what is the significance of Samuel Slater to this story of soccer? That Slater was not just the man who made the American textile industry successful, but the man who made it successful in Pawtucket. Without what he did, both in machine building and business managing, the soccer events of a century later might still have happened, but not where they did in New England.

The seeds had been planted. The American textile industry had begun in southeastern New England. Within a few decades, Pawtucket was no longer really a major player in that industry, at least not compared to other New England cities. But the fact that the industry had begun in that part of the country meant that it would grow in that part, even if not in exactly the same location. The trend that would make Fall River synonymous with both cotton and soccer had begun.

TO A GOOD DEGREE, Pawtucket was a victim of its own success when leadership of the new American textile industry moved to other parts of New England. In the early years of the 19th century, many of those new mills outside Pawtucket were started by men trained by Samuel Slater in Pawtucket (an extension of the way that Slater had been trained by Jedediah Strutt in Belper).[18]

The first of that expansion away from Pawtucket was to sites upstream on the Blackstone River, which flowed from central Massachusetts down into Rhode Island. Expansion also took place into the Pawtuxet River valley on the western side of Narragansett Bay, south of Providence.

At the same time, the industry's focus was changing from the mere production of cotton yarn to the weaving of that yarn into cotton cloth, an operation that had previously been done largely by home weavers but now was increasingly being moved into the mills.

The first major step toward a different part of New England from Pawtucket came in 1814, when a group of Boston businessmen established a cotton milling operation at Waltham, Mass., on the Charles River, just upstream from Boston. Investors discovered that the waterpower at Waltham was too limited, but the shortlived mills there were counted a success anyway, because techniques were developed there that the investors were able to put to profitable use elsewhere. The Waltham investors moved next into the Merrimack River valley north of Boston, near the New Hampshire state line, where there was much more waterpower.

This move to the Merrimack, although highly successful, with mills that lasted into the 20th century, did demonstrate one of the drawbacks of relying on waterpower, namely that you couldn't bring the energy to where you wanted it. You had to go where it happened to be. Where it was, in particular, was a falls on the Merrimack where the new town of Lowell, Mass., was created out of the wilderness (it may be difficult to think of Massachusetts as wilderness, but this was nearly 200 years ago). The mills of Lowell made it the dominant location of the textile industry for the first half of the 19th century, and a well publicized and misleading example of ideal conditions under which New England textile workers supposedly lived. Among the other locations to which the textile industry spread in these decades were Lawrence, Mass., and Manchester, N.H., both also on the Merrimack; Saco, Maine, on the Saco River; Holyoke, Mass., on the Connecticut River, and Lewiston, Maine, on the Androscoggin River. Each of these places developed as a textile center because of its proximity to waterpower. It was not until about 1850 that the first coal-fired steam engines began to become a factor in the textile industry.[19]

"Enlargement of mills and increase in investment brought a geographical shift," notes historian Caroline Ware, "drawing the bigger mills away from the small and easily dammed streams of Rhode Island and southern Massachusetts. The Pawtuxet Valley of Rhode Island had furnished ideal sites for the earliest mills, for the stream was small enough and had sufficient drop so that it could be dammed at frequent intervals with very little outlay of capital and slight engineering skill. Need for greater water power to turn more machinery and the possibility of accomplishing the difficult and costly feat of damming larger streams drew the later mills to the banks of the Merrimack and the Saco. The swift and abundant waters of those steams, furnishing power at Lowell, Manchester, Dover and Saco, did much to shift the principal seat of the industry to these northern New England towns."[20]

The movement of the textile industry away from Pawtucket was not entirely to the north, however. One of the places to which it expanded was Fall River.

STEAM IS a major part of what made Fall River the giant of the New England textile industry in the second half of the 19th century. It is not, however, what brought the textile industry to Fall River in the first place.

The textile mills of Fall River in the first half of the 19th century didn't compare with those of Lowell and other places where large mills burgeoned. However, there still was a place in the industry for the small mill.[21] This was fortunate for Fall River's entry into the business, for the waterpower available along the Quequechan was limited, and the Taunton River, by the time it flowed past Fall River en route to the sea, was too large for damming to power mills.

Fall River certainly had advantages, however. Steven Dunwell describes some of them in *Run of the Mill,* an overview of the 19th-century New England textile industry from the vantage point of 1978. Says Dunwell:

"Early mills at Fall River, then known as Troy, lined the Quequechan River in its short, precipitous drop from Watuppa Lake to the sea. The river's eight falls combined to make this the best tide-water priviledge in southern New England. It was perfect for industrialization—big enough for profit and expansion, yet small enough to be developed by local capital without interference from Boston. Here three local merchant-industrialists—Richard Borden, Bradford Durfee and Oliver Chace—established their manufacturing dynasties, concentrating particularly on print cloth while also developing iron making and shipping."[22] The fact that outside capital and outside oversight were not involved was to contribute to the eventual downfall of the Fall River textile business, but at this point it was an advantage.

Waterpower did not matter much in Fall River's later rise to the top of the cotton business, but during the waterpower era Fall River did have another advantage that was to remain important in the steam era. That was the moist climate that its seaside location gave it, a distinct boost to cotton manufacturing. The reason is that the manufacturing process creates static electricity that causes tangles, roughened surfaces and other difficulties with the yarn. Water is a good conductor of electricity, drawing the static electricity away from the yarn, so a moist atmosphere eases the troubles.[23] The brevity of this account belies the huge importance of this factor for the textile industry. Climate made Fall River and New Bedford ideal locations for cotton manufacturing, although even in those places artificial moisture was pumped into the mills.

The first cotton manufacturing operation in Fall River was the Globe Mill, started in 1811 by Oliver Durfee.[24] The Globe Mill was not a lasting success, however, and closed its doors in 1829. In 1813, two more mills were opened, both on the Quequechan, which the Globe Mill was not. The Troy Company, later renamed the Troy Cotton and Woolen Manufactory, and the Fall River Manufactory were the real point from which Fall River's textile industry grew.

Over the next four decades or so, more mills were regularly added, and while the Fall River textile industry grew steadily, it didn't threaten the powerhouses like Lowell and Lawrence. Then, in the middle of the 19th century, came steam, although its effects were not really felt until after the Civil War. When this happened, Fall River's seaside location (and later New Bedford's) became a gigantic advantage, because the coal that powered the steam engines that ran the mills could be brought in by ship nearly to the doorsteps of the mills. Inland sites like Lowell had to pay additional charges to get coal shipped by rail from Boston and other ports that were the closest to them. Fall River had already had a similar advantage as far as shipping in the raw cotton and shipping out the finished products, but when coal, considerably heavier and more expensive to ship than cotton, was added to the equation, the advantage was greatly multiplied.

It was no accident that the successful beginnings of the cotton industry in Fall River had occurred just after the War of 1812, in which Fall River had been blockaded by British ships. Similarly, the boom that was to make Fall River the textile capital of America—and maybe the world—took place in the first 15 years after the end of the Civil War.

The Civil War had a tremendous impact on the New England cotton manufacturing industry. The mills' supply of raw cotton from the South was practically shut off for four years. The demand for soldiers' uniforms turned to wool, and cotton manufacturing was retarded.[25]

A substantial factor in how particular mills fared during the war was how they dealt with their cotton inventories. Those, particularly at Lowell, that gambled on a short war and quickly used up those inventories took a bad financial blow.[26]

"The war left New England mills in a rearranged hierarchy," says Dunwell. "Those few mills that profited had a substantial head start on their competitors when prosperity returned. Wartime performance conditioned expansion during the boom years following Appomattox."

Additionally, Dunwell notes, the factors leading to postwar success also included the steam engine, which had finally come of age.[27]

IT TOOK A FEW YEARS after Appomattox for Fall River to build up speed, but by the early 1870s, it was experiencing a growth of the textile industry that has to be described as runaway. With that growth began an important surge of immigration from Britain, which had ended the ban on emigration of textile workers in 1825.

Dunwell describes that runaway expansion:

"Boom years following 1870 fueled the city's most dramatic expansion. Between 1871 and 1872, fifteen new corporations built twenty-two mills while their predecessors extended their own operations. By 1876, Fall River's forty-three factories had an installed capacity of well over one million spindles [these spools, onto which finished yarn is wound in the spinning process, are the basic yardstick of the textile industry], feeding yarn to more than 30,000 looms. Fall River grew faster than any other textile city of its time. One out of every four new spindles added to New England between 1850 and 1875 was placed in Fall River. The city controlled one-sixth of all New England cotton capacity, and one-half of all print cloth production. Fall River rightly called itself "Spindle City"—preeminent in America, second only to Manchester, England, in the world.

"Fall River's astonishing growth reflected a single-minded purpose. Seven-eighths of the urban labor force worked in textiles."[28]

Fall River historian Philip Silvia notes that "By 1880, five spindles existed [in Fall River] for every one at war's end."[29]

During the same period, the "urban labor force" grew as remarkably as did the number of mills. Between 1865 and 1885, the population of Fall River more than tripled, from 17,481 to 56,870.[30] A very large part of that population growth consisted of immigrants from the textile manufacturing cities of Lancashire. The early 1870s are when Fall River became the destination of choice for immigrant textile workers, a city as totally identified with that industry as, decades later, Pittsburgh was with steel or Detroit with automobiles.

"THESE TOWNS to which British textile workers flocked by the shipload in the 1860s were not unlike those they had left," says Maldwyn Jones, an historian of the American melting pot, in *Destination America*. "Roused from bed at six each morning by the familiar sound of the mill whistle, Lancashire and Yorkshire immigrants gazed out at forests of chimneys, acres of brick and granite factories and rows of houses. Among the spindles and shuttles they were surrounded by old neighbors speaking familiar dialects. It must have been difficult to believe they were not still in England. . . . Fall River was a bastion of Lancashire culture. Folk there still indulged their passion for football and dialect recitations, their taste for black puddings, pork pies, tripe and cowheel. To complete the illusion of being in Lancashire one could even see housewives on their knees scrubbing and whitening the front doorstep."[31]

Indeed, the thousands of immigrants from Lancashire to Fall River tried, successfully, to replicate what they had known on the other side of the ocean. One of the elements of that, by the late 1870s, was association football.

Football played by the "association rules" or "London rules" formulated in 1863 seems to have made its appearance in Lancashire about 10 years later, aided by the sons of mill owners who had attended upper-class schools and learned what, before the 1870s, was largely an upper-class game.

According to *The Oxford Companion to World Sports and Games*, the coming to Lancashire of association football occured first in the village of Turton, between Blackburn and Bolton, where matches under the Harrow school's rules had been played for many years before the local leaders decided in 1872 to actually form a football club. Two years later, Turton decided to change from the Harrow rules to the London rules that had been drawn up at the Freemasons' Tavern in 1863. Soon, other clubs were formed in Blackburn, Bolton, Darwen and elsewhere, and the Lancashire Football Association was formed in 1878.[32]

The most famous of the early Lancashire teams is Blackburn Rovers, which is probably the oldest soccer club in the world to still be competing at a very high professional level today. The team finished fifth in the English Premier League in 2003, 128 years after its founding in 1875 by former students of the Blackburn Grammar School. Blackburn Rovers hired their first professional player in 1880, and won the English Football Association Cup in 1884, 1885 and 1886, thus becoming the first team to really dominate that famous competition.[33]

The other particularly strong team of the very earliest years of Lancashire soccer, Darwen Football Club, which also was founded in 1875, hasn't been in the professional levels of the sport for more than a century, but it was still there in the 1890s, when it was a member of the Football League. Perhaps nothing shows the early influence of Lancashire on the sport more than the fact that of the 12 founding members in 1888 of the Football League, the world's first professional soccer league, five were from Lancashire. The Lancashire teams in that first league season included the first champion, Preston North End.

Relatively unnoticed among the early Lancashire teams is one that was to become far and away the best-known soccer team in England, and perhaps the world, Manchester United. It was founded by railway workers in 1878 as Newton Heath Football Club, nicknamed "The Heathens."[34]

These early Lancashire teams weren't merely replicas of the upper-class amateur teams of southern England. Notes the *Oxford Companion,* "When Blackburn Olympic visited Kensington Oval in 1883 and beat the Old Etonians in the Cup final, they included in their team several working lads: spinners and weavers from the cotton trade of Lancashire, a picture framer, a moulder's mate, a dentist's assistant . . ."[35]

Soccer in Lancashire clearly was filtering down to the sort of men who were making the decision to emigrate to America. And America, to Lancashire men of that day, meant Fall River.

The English were not the first immigrant group to be attracted by the textile mills of New England, nor were they, in the 1870s, the only one. The Portuguese immigration for which the area was to become noted was still in the future, but the native Americans who had worked the mills in the early part of the century had long since been joined—some said supplanted—by immigrants, particularly Irish and French-Canadian.

The French-Canadians, who were many in number, brought no soccer traditions with them, nor, at one time, did the Irish, many of whom had originally come to the New England textile towns as laborers building the mills. By the 1870s and 1880s, however, these were a different sort of Irish immigrants in places like Fall River, people who had come to America not directly from Ireland, but by way of Lancashire,[36] where they had become steeped not just in the ways of the textile business, but in the ways of Lancashire, including football.

There were several important factors in the emigration of Lancashire textile workers to Fall River beyond the simple lure of America and the higher wages that were supposed to be available in Fall River mills.

In 1825, Britain had ended its restrictions on the emigration of textile workers, the restrictions that had forced Samuel Slater and others like him to leave for America without fanfare. From then until 1885, when the United States passed the Contract Labor Law, preventing companies in most industries from hiring workers overseas before they came to America, the New England textile mills were free to recruit workers in Lancashire.

"During the 'cotton famine' brought on by the American Civil War blockade," says Rowland Berthoff in *British Immigrants in Industrial America*, "unemployed English operatives clamored for assistance to emigrate, while the American labor shortage [caused by workers being drafted] led Northern manufacturers to recruit hands in Scotland and England."[37]

American companies weren't the only ones urging Lancashire's textile "operatives," as mill workers were called on both sides of the Atlantic, to emigrate to America. In many cases, their own unions were doing likewise.

Those unions, according to Maldwyn Jones, saw emigration of certain of their members as a way to ease distress in the textile industry of Lancashire. Thinning out the ranks in Lancashire textile mills would be of benefit to both those who departed and those who stayed behind. The result was that many unions provided assistance for unemployed members to emigrate.[38]

Despite the fact that conditions in New England textile mills and New England textile towns were far from ideal, the move may, indeed, have been particularly beneficial to some of those who went, men who had been blacklisted by Lancashire textile companies for union activity. In a 1979 study of the industrial communities of Fall River and Lynn, Mass., historian John Cumbler states: "Lancashire unions began setting aside funds for the emigration of workers as early as 1837, but it was not until the second half of the nineteenth century that these funds affected emigration to the United States. Throughout the 1870s and 1880s and continuing into the twentieth century, Lancashire textile unions provided money for blacklisted or 'victimized' members to emigrate. Many chose to come to Fall River."[39]

Textile mill owners in Fall River and elsewhere in New England did view English operatives with particular wariness, because they were much more likely to form unions than workers of other nationalities. In part, this was simply because unions were not a new idea to men who had had previous exposure to them in Lancashire, but in many instances, the fact that they were men inclined to union activity was a large part of the reason why they were in America at all.

Over its decades as a textile manufacturing center, Fall River had a contentious labor history. That many of the leaders of Fall River textile workers' unions, particularly in the more skilled trades like spinning and weaving, were English, was no happenstance.

THE CONNECTION between Fall River and Lancashire was duplicated on a smaller scale, but perhaps a more frantic one, in the connection between Paterson, N.J., the center of the American silk industry, and Macclesfield, England, the center of the English silk industry.

The event that particularly accelerated this took place in 1860, when the Cobden Treaty between Great Britain and France eliminated all tariffs on the importation of manufactured silk products from France to Britain, badly damaging the English silk industry.[40] The movement of immigrants from Macclesfield to Paterson turned from a trickle to a flood. Within a few decades, these immigrants were bringing an interest in soccer with them. Macclesfield, although not in Lancashire, was not that far away, and shared in the growth of soccer that took place in Lancashire in the 1870s and 1880s. Macclesfield Town Football Club, which currently is a member of the English Third Division, was founded in 1874.

The movement from Macclesfield to Paterson was even more stunning that that from Lancashire to New England. Berthoff describes it in some detail:

"Nearly the whole English silk industry migrated to America after the Civil War. . . . Free-trade dogma wrecked silk in Great Britain just when the United States switched to a protective tariff; during the Civil War the duties on silk more than doubled. As the favored industry prospered after 1865, operatives swarmed in from Macclesfield, Coventry and lesser silk towns of England and Scotland. Owners of British factories crated their machinery and left for New Jersey [by now, exportation of textile machinery was legal] with their workmen. . . .

"Earlycomers assisted friends at home to join them, while the Macclesfield unions sent others. Their belongings filled the Paterson depot. . . .

"It has been estimated that between 1870 and 1893 about fifteen thousand Macclesfielders, as well as many Frenchmen, emigrated to Paterson. . . . In Macclesfield, men spoke of Paterson as familiarly as if it were only a run of half an hour by train."[41]

By 1893, clearly, a considerable interest in association football also had emigrated to Paterson somewhere in that crowd of Macclesfielders. The following year, Paterson True Blues reached the final of the American Football Association Cup for the first time.

IT SEEMS OBVIOUS that there was a connection between football in Lancashire textile centers and football in New England textile centers, particularly Fall River. However, it would be misleading to turn a blind eye to the fact that those American textile centers were not places that easily lent themselves to leisure-time activities, although in the case of football they somehow did. Those English textile operatives who clamored to emigrate to America might not have done so quite so loudly if they had better understood what conditions were like in New England.

Consider Steve Dunwell's gruesome description of Lawrence, Mass. (not Fall River, but not necessarily much worse) around the turn of the century:

". . . massive European immigration between 1890 and 1912 combined with declining industrial conditions to produce an unusually desperate environment. Housing went from bad to worse as multistory wooden tenements were thrown up to accommodate the surge of immigrants. Tenements rose higher each decade, crowding so close together that a housewife could hang her pots and pans on the outside wall of the adjoining tenement. Apartments offered few amenities, and even windows were a luxury. Increased rents . . . forced most families to take in boarders and fill every room with beds. Even the kitchen—the social center of the apartment and the only source of heat—served double duty as a bedroom. Privacy was nonexistent. As immigrants were packed tighter and tighter into the slums of central Lawrence, population density soared to over one hundred persons per acre. At the center of the immigrant area, density reached six hundred per acre . . .

"Health inspectors reported a 'fearful mortality' stalking the immigrant districts of mill cities, deemed 'hotbeds of disease.' Crowded, unventilated apartments bred tuberculosis. A 'poisonous miasma' surrounded the privies between tenements, combining with polluted river and canal water to add typhoid and cholera to the list of mill city scourges. Waves of disease swept down the Merrimack, as one city after another drank water contaminated by mill workers upstream and passed their recontaminated wastes down the river. Disease followed the immigrant cycle, striking destitute newcomers with special virulence."[42]

Was Fall River any better? Maybe, but not by much according to a description of the tenements of the Borden Mills. A concerned churchman of the same era, William Bayard Hale, is quoted by Cumbler. Hale said:

"Operatives live in bedrooms and kitchens. . . . The population of the court is about one thousand. . . . Looking in at entries, the plastering of the walls is seen to be discolored and broken and the stairs bare and dilapidated. The court is littered with refuse; one threads one's way among unsavory heaps. Along under the eaves of every block is a ridge composed of potato parings, egg shells and garbage; the universal rule is to pour the kitchen emptyings out the window.

"The court is the playground for the children and the thoroughfare for all. In certain details of filth, it is probably not matched outside of Fall River anywhere in what we call civilization. And in the center stands a pump. The air is pestilential and the place revolting to every sense. The heart sickens at the sight of the crowds who sit on stoops and hang out windows and gaze at their misery. . . .

". . . You see many blocks worse than those of the Borden Mills. 'Little Canada,' the property of the American Linen Mills Company, is unspeakable. The Slade Mill tenements stand in a swamp. . . . "[43]

In a living atmosphere like this, it seems no wonder that children were eager accomplices in efforts by both parents and mill owners to get them into the mills as young as possible, regardless of child-labor laws.

But those mills were no picnic either, as immigrants from Lancashire discovered. The main difference between New England textile mills and Lancashire textile mills was that the operatives were required to work at a much faster rate in New England. Spinning machinery was operated by the mills at a greater speed than in Lancashire and weavers were required to tend a larger number of the automated looms.[44] And the atmosphere in which they did this, with artificial moisture added to the natural humidity, was almost as dismal as that in the tenements.

T.M. Young was an English newspaperman familiar with Lancashire mills who wrote a book titled *The American Cotton Industry* after a tour of American textile cities around the turn of the century. Of Fall River mills in general, he observed: "In the mills, the air is, as a rule, very bad, and there is often no provision at all for proper ventilation. In many mills I have seen the condensed moisture streaming down the windows, and clouds of water vapour, almost scalding hot, rising amongst the looms from open grids on the floor. On the whole, I should say that the conditions in which factory labour is performed, even at this temperate season [April] and in this model State, are very much more trying to human endurance and health than in Lancashire."[45]

Of workers in one Fall River mill in particular, the Chace Mill, Young said: "The faces of the weavers looked pinched and sallow, and the arms of many of them were pitifully thin. I do not care how many dollars a week those people may have been earning; they were badly off."[46]

In addition, says a historian of more recent vintage, Berthoff, many of the newly arrived English workers saw the American mills as tyrannical. In England, individual operatives' rates of production had been kept private between them and the company, but in Fall River, Berthoff notes, the operatives were spurred on to outproduce each other by slates chalked with each man's record for all to see.[47]

It was not the sort of setting in which one would ordinarily expect any sort of athletic activity to flourish, but it did.

IN INCREASING NUMBERS by the 1870s, the cotton workers of Lancashire were looking to Fall River and the silk workers of Macclesfield were looking to Paterson. Also by that decade, the thread workers of Paisley, Scotland, were looking to Kearny, N.J., and Pawtucket, R.I. But unlike their English counterparts, they were preceded to America by the companies they worked for in Britain.

Paisley, in the Clyde valley just downstream from Glasgow, was, without any doubt, the world center of the cotton thread-making industry. The two giants of the industry, the Clark Thread Mills and J&P Coats, both were located there, as were a number of smaller companies. By the middle of the 19th century, all had been attracted by America.

The making of cotton thread hadn't begun quite as early as the making of cotton cloth. This was fortunate for the growth of the thread-making business in Kearny and Pawtucket. Thread-making didn't have to come to America in the piecemeal, sometimes clandestine fashion that cotton manufacturing had, because by the time it was ready to make that leap, Britain no longer had laws preventing textile workers and textile machinery from leaving that country.

The event that inspired the invention of cotton thread took place in 1806, when Napoleon took over the German port of Hamburg, temporarily cutting British textile manufacturers off from the supply of silk used by weavers as guide thread on looms. Within a few years, Patrick Clark of Paisley had invented a substitute, twisting cotton yarn together to create a sufficiently strong thread of cotton. The Clark Mill, manufacturing cotton thread, opened in Paisley in 1812.[48]

The rival that eventually outstripped Clark in the thread-making business joined the competition in 1826 when James Coats started a nearby mill. Four years later, he retired and left the business to his sons James and Peter, hence the name J&P Coats.[49]

By the 1850s, the thread-makers of Paisley had developed a huge new market for their product: women needing thread for sewing their families' clothes in their own homes following the invention of the sewing machine. A considerable portion of this market was in America, and both the Clark company and the Coats company had sales agents in the United States. For both, the next step was to begin making thread in America, so that they could sell it there without having to pay tariffs to get it there. Both made their moves shortly after the end of the Civil War.

Clark selected Newark, N.J., as the site for its American mill. The Clark Thread Company was incorporated by the state of New Jersey in 1865, and by 1866 it had opened its first mill in the northern part of Newark, across the Passaic River from Kearny.[50] Newark had none of the advantages traditionally associated with textile manufacturing. The Passaic River offered no waterpower at that point, having done most of its dropping already, particularly at Paterson, but the moist coast was still about 20 miles away. What Newark did have included a moderate tax rate and access to an excellent transportation network. Railroads were becoming a more important factor in American life, and Newark was located near New York and along railroad lines connecting New York with Philadelphia and the west and south, negating the fact that Newark, at least this part of it, was too far upriver for oceangoing ships.

A few years later, Coats made its move to America, but in a slightly different fashion. In 1869, it went into partnership with a Pawtucket firm, the Conant Thread Company, that had been founded just the year before. Conant immediately began making J&P Coats thread in Pawtucket.[51]

Both companies expanded their American production quickly. The Coats/Conant operation in Pawtucket built four additional mills, all on the same property as the original mill, in 1869, 1873, 1875 and 1881.[52] That property was several miles from the Blackstone River, where the American textile industry had been born in the 1790s, but this was a new era in the textile business and waterpower was unnecessary. All of those mills were powered by steam engines. In New Jersey, Clark's expansion was not on its original site. In 1880, it expanded across the Passaic River into the East Newark section of Kearny in a big way. It built a second thread-making operation there (which, like the Newark complex, included a mill for making spools), and it purchased the Mile End Spool Cotton Mill in Kearny, which had been opened by Mile End, yet another Scottish firm, in 1876.[53] The two mills were adjacent to each other, the new Clark mills immediately north of the Mile End mill.

Both of these thread-making operations, Clark in Kearny and Coats in Pawtucket, were well established by the time the United States' Contract Labor Law changed things in 1885 for those companies' ability to bring employees directly from Scotland. Until then, Clark and Coats had been able to hire for their new American operations people who had already been working for them in Paisley, and the Scottish populations of both Kearny and Pawtucket had grown sharply, with particularly Kearny starting on the way to its "Little Scotland" reputation.

Rowland Berthoff comments that once it began operations in New Jersey "most of Clark's employees during the rest of the century hailed from Paisley."[54] *The Harvard Encyclopedia of American Ethnic Groups* says of the same period: "Scottish thread-manufacturing firms set up branches in America and staffed them with experienced workers from their factories at home."[55] After 1885, those immigrants from Paisley had to wait until they got to America before signing up to work for Clark in Kearny or Coats in Pawtucket.

Those Scottish immigrants were as likely to bring association football traditions with them as were immigrants from Lancashire. Football, which had flourished in its disorganized forms in Scotland in earlier years, reappeared not long after the formulation of the association rules in London in 1863, according to *The Encyclopedia of World Soccer*. The process, it says, was somewhat similar to the process that brought football back to Lancashire, using students as a conduit. Returning students brought the new soccer rules north to Glasgow, and rugby rules to Edinburgh. It notes that "The first Scottish club, Queen's Park Football Club, was formed on the south side of Glasgow in 1867 by members of the Y.M.C.A. who had gathered regularly in Queen's Park to play pickup games."[56]

Scotland was behind England in the formation of the game, but not far behind, ten years (1857 to 1867) in the founding of the first club, ten years (1863 to 1873) in the founding of the football association, and two years (1888 to 1890) in the founding of the first professional league. Tactically, it may have been ahead, for around 1870 it made a critical contribution to the evolution of the way the game was played. In England, the standard way of advancing the ball upfield was for one player to dribble it forward, but Scottish teams pioneered the tactic of moving it forward by passing it from one player to another. The fact that Scottish soccer was a bit more innovative than English was one reason why English clubs often looked toward Scotland when they became interested in hiring professional players.

The local professional team in Paisley is the St. Mirren Football Club. That club, which was one of the original members of the Scottish League and still plays in the Scottish first division today, was founded in 1874.

Names of early competitors in the American Football Association Cup tournament, like Kearny Rangers, Paterson Rangers and Newark Caledonians, certainly imply that the Scottish workers coming to New Jersey around 1880 were bringing soccer with them. Rangers was a very frequently used name in American ethnic soccer for Scottish-based teams, just like Kickers for German teams, Inter for Italian teams and Falcons for Polish teams. In Pawtucket, where J&P Coats sponsored a team in the first American

Soccer League of the 1920s, that team, after Coats ended its sponsorship, reverted to its original name, Pawtucket Rangers.

CLARK WAS the dominant employer in Kearny in the 1880s, but it was by no means the only one. In 1881, the Marshall Linen Mills, from Ireland, began operation just north of the Clark/Mile End complex. And in 1886, they were joined by another Scottish-based firm, the Nairn Linoleum Company.

Nairn was located in Kirkaldy, on the North Sea side of Scotland, and soccer didn't arrive there as early as it had in Paisley. The local professional team, Raith Rovers, which also plays today in the Scottish first division, wasn't founded until 1883, a few years after Nairn began producing linoleum in Kirkaldy.

The company was founded by Michael Nairn, a Kirkaldy businessman who, in 1838, began making canvas cloth that was sold to English floorcloth manufacturers to be used as backing for floorcoverings. He soon decided, according to the Congoleum Corporation, the successor to Nairn Linoleum, that his firm's best hope for success was to make the backing into floorcovering there in Kirkaldy, rather than sell it to English manufacturers.[57]

The making of floorcovering involved stretching the canvas on a frame and then trowelling specially mixed paint onto both sides of the canvas, drying it and then printing designs onto it, a process that took about 10 months.

Michael Nairn died in 1858 and his son, Michael Barker Nairn, began running the firm, then named Michael Nairn & Company, and making considerable improvements in it. One of those improvements was to expand the line of products the company was making, and by the late 1870s, that line included linoleum.

This new type of floorcovering, whose main ingredient was the oil of flax or linseed oil, had been invented in 1863 by Englishman Frederick Walton, who named it by combining the Latin words for flax and oil.[58]

According to Congoleum, Michael Barker Nairn did a great deal of research into the manfacturing processes of linoleum, and thus was ready to enter that field when Walton's patent on linoleum expired.

"In 1886, Michael Barker Nairn set off on a trip to America," Congoleum says. "The object of this visit was to buy land on which he intended to build a linoleum factory. He recognized the market in the USA and felt that since there was only one manufacturer there at this time, he could establish a profitable business. By August 1886, the Nairn Linoleum Company had been set up in Kearny, East Newark in the state of New Jersey."[59]

Nairn was aided in this move by the fact that linoleum, as an industry that was as yet undeveloped in the United States, was exempted from the provisions of the Contract Labor Law of 1885. Thread-making companies such as Clark were no longer allowed to bring employees over from their Scottish plants, but a few blocks away, Nairn faced no such restriction.

According to New Jersey state statistics collected by Kearny resident James Waller, Nairn became Kearny's second largest employer of Scottish workers, trailing only Clark, by 1909. Within the following decade, however, both were swamped in that category by the Federal Shipyard, started on the Hackensack River side of Kearny by the U.S. Steel Corporation during World War I.[60]

THE ARRIVAL of companies in varied businesses like textiles, linoleum and shipbuilding meant that Kearny was not a one-industry town, and its next-door neighbor Harrison was even more diversified. The same cannot be said of Fall River, which was completely tied to the textile industry by the 1870s, and certainly not of New Bedford, which performed the amazing (and ultimately self-defeating) accomplishment of successfully converting from being a one-industry city in one business to being a one-industry city in another after the failure of the first.

The first textile mill in New Bedford that stayed in business for more than a few years was the Wamsutta (a local Indian name), which didn't open until 1848. After that, it was 1871 before the second, the Potamska, began. Obviously, New Bedford was exceedingly slow in getting into the textile business, far behind Fall River. What eventually pushed it into textiles was the collapse of its one industry, whaling, a process that began in 1859 and extended into the 1870s.

In the 1840s and '50s, New Bedford wasn't just a whaling city, it was *the* whaling city. A relatively small port on an ocean that was ringed by large cities managed to dominate the industry. Indirectly, New Bedford's whaling industry had an effect on the eventual soccer history of southeastern New England. Although the immigration of Portuguese-speaking people was not a factor in the earliest stirrings of soccer in southeastern New England, before 1900, events of New Bedford's whaling era are the reason why southeastern New England later became a focus of Portuguese immigration and New England soccer was so filled with Portuguese players by 1950. Whaling ships from New Bedford often took on crew members in the Azores, islands in mid-Atlantic 700 miles west of Portugal that were a part of Portugal, and Cape Verde, islands off the coast of West Africa that were a Portuguese possession. From this came the first trickle of Portuguese immigration into New England.[61]

The beginning of the end for the whaling industry, at least as it was known in the mid-19th century, came in 1859, when oil was discovered near Titusville, Pa., sparking the first regular extraction of oil from the ground for commercial purposes. "Up to the latter part of the nineteenth century whale and sperm oil were important sources of fuel for lighting and lubricating purposes," says historian Seymour Wolfbein in *Decline of a Cotton Textile City: A Study of New Bedford.* "Their price was high, however, and led to a search for substitute fuels. . . . The finishing blow was dealt when petroleum was discovered in Pennsylvania, sharply restricting the market for the important products of New Bedford's whaling industry."[62] The market for whale oil didn't immediately dry up after 1859, but it started in that direction.

The next event that sent the New Bedford whaling fleet reeling was the Civil War. Not only were 50 New Bedford whaling ships victimized by Confederate crusiers, but another 37 New Bedford whalers became what was known as the "Stone Fleet," ships deliberately sunk at the entrances to Southern ports as part of the Northern effort to blockade those ports.[63] The *coup de grace* came in the 1870s. In both 1871 and 1876, parts of the New Bedford whaling fleet were crushed in Arctic ice, when the open-water gap between the Alaskan coast and offshore ice floes closed unexpectedly. In 1871, 32 ships were lost, and in 1876, 12 more were.[64] If the market for whale oil had still been as brisk as it had been 20 years before, perhaps New Bedford whaling could have recovered from the ice, but it never did. The industry did struggle on into the 20th century (losing five more ships to the ice in 1888), but even with inflation, the earnings of New Bedford's now-tiny whaling fleet in 1916 were less than one-thirtieth of what they had been in 1857, the industry's peak.[65]

And so New Bedford turned, reluctantly, to textiles. If the events that meant the end of the New Bedford whaling business had happened fifty years earlier, textiles might never have caught on in New Bedford, which was almost completely without waterpower. By the 1870s, that didn't matter. Even so, New Bedford was not quick to scramble into the textile business. The next new company after the Potamska Mills in 1871 was the Acushnet Mills in 1881. In the course of this slow growth, New Bedford found its niche in the textile industry. By the start of the 20th century, it had become known for specializing in producing a finer grade of material than the print cloth that was Fall River's forte.[66] A sign of that niche remains today, at least in name. Although they haven't been produced in New Bedford for decades, Wamsutta sheets are still a popular brand.

If the 1870s had been the years when the textile industry took off in Fall River, the following three decades were New Bedford's growth years. "After hesitating for another ten years and enduring another Arctic catastrophe," New Bedford historian Daniel Georgianna says in *The Strike of '28*, "the majority of whaling merchants abandoned the now high-risk and low-profit whaling industry and quickly moved to the safe six or eight percent dividend from textiles. From 1881 to the beginning of World War I, 32 cotton manufacturing companies were incorporated, worth $100,000,000 and employing 30,000 people. During the first third of the twentieth century, until the industry's collapse during the Great Depression of the 1930s, about 90 percent of the city's manufacturing employees worked in cotton mills. New Bedford continued as a one-industry town, simply switching from whaling to textiles."[67]

COTTON THRIVED in both Fall River and New Bedford in the early years of the 20th century, but by the time of World War I, industry leaders in both cities had made a string of decisions during those peak years that they would later regret and the growing southern textile industry would appreciate. From the vantage point of the 21st century, it may seem obvious that there were clouds on the horizon, but it wasn't obvious then.

The most important of those decisions had to do with the selection of machinery for the mills. It is only natural for a new factory, as the textile mills of the South were in the latter part of the 19th century, to select the latest machinery for the start of its operations. But northern mill owners, particularly in Fall River, increased the problem by insisting on clinging to outdated machinery. Says Dunwell:

"Too many mill owners bet against the inexorable advance of technology—and lost. Automation was in fact inevitable. Management found false security in its long-lived but old-fashioned machines, which kept on producing long after they became obsolete. As new installations were increasingly concentrated outside New England, the region found itself surfeited with antique machines. In 1928, a typically conservative New Bedford mill had no looms or spindles less than twenty-five years old. Henry Ford bought some of their machines for his museum!"[68]

The clouds on the horizon were there, if only the mill owners could have seen them through the fog created by their cotton centennials and dividend checks. "As it turned out," says Wolfbein, "by the time many of the mills awoke to the fact that their equipment was obsolete, it was too late."[69]

Not helping matters any was the way that mills, particularly in Fall River, had developed a network of interlocking directorates, which also included the local banks. A similar, although smaller, web existed in New Bedford, but the Fall River network, based heavily on the involvements of founding families of that city's textile industry such as the Bordens and Durfees, made it particularly ill-suited to resist southern competition.

That elaborate system of interlocking directorships of Fall River's most important corporations and institutions enabled the Borden family dynasty to dominate scores of smaller investors and manfacturers.[70]

Said T.M. Young at the time, with a perceptive outsider's eye: "Mr. M.C.D. Borden . . . is a paramount power in the cotton trade of Fall River. In the matter of wages he acts independently of the other manufacturers, who have sometimes been compelled to follow his lead when it was exceedingly inconvenient for them to do so."[71]

The result was a situation that made it easy for those clouds on the horizon to be obscured, or at least not acted upon. There probably were men in Fall River who recognized what the future held, who saw that the slowly growing southern textile industry would someday constitute a serious challenge to New England. If there were, they must have been men who were frozen out of real influence by the interlocking power structure of Fall River.

Those advantages held by southern mill owners were substantial, whether the northern mill owners could see them or not. These included proximity to raw materials (meaning both cotton and coal), abundant low-priced labor, freedom from legal restrictions, cheap hydroelectric power, the latest equipment, low taxes and a large home market.[72]

Some in New England may have been alarmed, but apparently not the solemnent mill owners, who failed to take notice. Their attitude is echoed by Melvin Copeland, an historian not known for being particularly critical of the industry, writing in 1912: "Till 1880 the cotton manufacturing supremacy of New England was not threatened. But when mills began to spring up in the South like mushrooms, grave fears were entertained for the future of the industry in the section where it had first taken root. These fears have now almost entirely disappeared, since by readjustment and economy the New England manufacturers have given evidence of being able to keep their foothold."[73] Disaster for New England mills was only a decade away, but many shared Copeland's view that their troubles were behind them.

EVENTS OF the 17th, 18th and 19th centuries, political and economic, had set the stage for the arrival of soccer in New England and New Jersey. Events of the late 19th century also set the stage for soccer's departure, but that was still many decades in the future.

II

The Era of the
American Football
Association

IT MAY NOT HAVE BEEN the birthplace of American soccer, but it would be true to say that the birthplace of the organizational side of American soccer was Odgen Street in the northern section of Newark, N.J. There, one evening in the summer of 1884, a group of men, primarily from Newark and Kearny, met to found the American Football Association, the first "national" soccer organization in the United States.

The best window into the activities of pre-World War I American soccer is the Spalding Guides, a series of annual review and preview publications. The 1910–11 issue contains a description of that occasion:

"In 1884, the American Football Association was organized at a meeting held in the Clark Thread Company's hose house in Ogden Street. A subscription was opened and the sum of $500 was raised among prominent business men and admirers of the game in Newark, East Newark, New York and Paterson. The Clark Thread Company also contributed liberally to the fund. The following officers were elected: James Grant, president; Thomas B. Hood, vice-president; Robert L. Craig, treasurer; John Wexton and Peter J. O'Toole, secretaries. It was decided to hold an annual competition and to offer a silver cup to be known as the American Football Association Challenge Cup, the winner of the final round each year to be presented with the cup by the Association and the name of the winning club to be suitably inscribed on the trophy."[1]

The article then notes that in that first season of the AFA, 13 teams entered the cup competition, Almas, Tiffany Rovers, Thistles, Domestics and Riversides of Newark; ONT and Kearny Rangers of Kearny; New York FC and New York Thistles of New York City; Paterson FC of Paterson; Ansonia FC of Ansonia, Conn., and Fall River Rovers and Fall River East Ends of Fall River, Mass.[2]

The American Football Association performed some of the same function that the original Football Association had in England in 1863, standardizing of the rules. James Robinson writes about some of this function in his 1966 doctoral dissertation, *The History of Soccer in the City of St. Louis.* In particular, Robinson notes that the AFA introduced several features that have continued to this day, such as penalty kicks, allowing the referee to award free kicks without waiting for appeal, putting nets on the goals and one that seems painfully obvious today but wasn't always, prohibiting referees from placing bets on the game.[3]

ONT, which has sometimes been listed as having been from Newark rather than Kearny, won that first tournament, by beating the New York FC, 2–1, in the final on April 25, 1885, and thus can be called the first champion of American soccer. ONT was the team sponsored by the Clark Thread Company. The initials stood for "Our New Thread," a product name that was to last well into the 20th century, and adorned the Clark mill's gigantic smokestack in Kearny.

ONT, which originally was for Clark employees only, was formed on Nov. 11, 1883. The first game, in Harrison on Dec. 2, 1883, was an intramural one, rather than against another club, with the membership divided into teams in a way that was not unusual in sports of that day. The score was Married Men 4, Single Men 2.

Two good things happened to ONT as a result of its victory in the first AFA Cup final. One was that ONT was invited to make an 11-game tour of Canada a few months later, although, as with the United States, the definition of "Canada" in terms of its national soccer federation was limited to a relatively small region of the country. Canada at that time meant the Western Football Association, organized in 1880, with membership confined to southern Ontario. The other reason was that five ONT players were chosen for the United States team that faced Canada (again the WFA) in November 1885 in the first full international ever played by the United States. (However, the U.S. Soccer Federation does not recognize this game as having been a full international, both because of the limited geographic range of the American Football Association and because it happened before the USSF was founded in 1913.)

That Canadian tour took the ONT team though a number of soccer hotbeds of southern Ontario, where it played the leading teams of Toronto, Dundas, Berlin (now Kitchener) and Galt. ONT won nine games on the tour, lost one and tied one. That tie, a 1–1 stalemate, was particularly significant because it came against Berlin Rangers, the champion of Canada.[4]

The international game was part of a trip to the New York area in which the Canadian team played several games against American elevens, including the first indoor soccer games ever recorded. The United States-Canada game took place on Nov. 27, 1885, the day after Thanksgiving, and was reported in the following day's *New York Times*. The headline used the term "picked team," an early expression meaning an all-star selection from among more than one club (four clubs in the case of this American selection). These were not really the champion teams of the two countries as the story called them. Under the headlines "Canadians The Victors" and "The Picked American Football Team Beaten," the *Times* report said:

"The football match yesterday between the champion elevens of Canada and of the United States, played acording to the American Association rules, on the grounds of the O.N.T. Athletic Association, at East Newark, was one of the best contested games ever seen in this neighborhood. The Canadians won, but only after a hard fight. The play was very rough at times, so much so that the referee had to interfere several times. Once two of the players indulged in a regular fist fight. The home team had been well selected and played well together, considering they had no practice as a team. About 2,000 people were present, some 60 of whom were ladies.

"The ball was kicked off by the home team punctually at 3 o'clock. Both sides played up well and no advantage was scored until [Alex] Gibson of the Canadian team, got the ball near the touch line and dribbled it up to the goal posts and shot it through. Several times after this the Canadian goal was saved by [John] McKendrick, who was ably assisted by [Solomon] Brubacher and Holden [this is an error, Harry Holden was one of the American players]. The forwards of the mixed team did good service toward the latter part of the game, but were unable to get a goal, the Canadians at the call of time having scored the only goal made."[5]

The five ONT players on the United States team all had made the trip to Canada earlier in the year. They were goalkeeper Patrick Hughes, fullback Harry Holden, halfback Joe Swithenby, and forwards Jack Swithenby and J. McGurck. The others were fullback J. Lennox of Kearny Rangers, halfback J. Hood of Kearny Rangers, halfback W. Turner of Paterson Thistles, forward Young of Kearny Rangers, forward A. Turner of Paterson Thistles and forward Lucas of Newark Almas. Several American soccer traditions were started in this game. One of them was the habit followed by newspapers for many decades of often omitting the first names of players (but including the first names of referees, because they were "gentlemen").

ONT won the American Football Association Cup again in 1886 and 1887. In both years, Kearny Rangers were the runnerup. ONT won the final by 3–1 in 1886 and 3–2 in 1887. There was no Canadian trip in 1886, but there was another visit by a Canadian team, a selection from five Ontario clubs, to New Jersey. Again, the United States and Canada played at Clark Field, but this time the game was on Thanksgiving Day itself, and one of the teams, the Canadians, had eaten Thanksgiving dinner not long before the game, a bit heavier than an ideal pregame meal. This time, the *Newark Evening News* carried a report on the game, under the headlines "The Canadians Beaten" and "A Sharp Foot Ball Game in the Wind and Rain." It stated:

"Fast falling rain was making a big marsh of the foot ball grounds in Kearny yesterday afternoon when the members of the Canadian foot ball team, dressed in their showy uniforms, made their appearance. The citizens of the Dominion arrived in the city shortly after noon. By the time they had shaken hands with all their friends and had eaten dinner at the Continental Hotel it was nearly 3 o'clock. Most people supposed that the game would be postponed on account of the miserable weather, but the Canadian players found the American team practicing and ready to receive them while 2,000 enthusiasts stood shivering in the rain anxious to witness the contest. The ground was soft and slippery, and the spot where the spectators stood was a little lake. The dead heads, who were perched on the surrounding fences and freight cars, had by far the better view of the game, and they saw it in more comfort. The game was soon called, Robert Craig being chosen for referee, with H. Starmer, of the Almas, umpire for the Americans, and William Clark Jr. for the Canadians.

"The Canadians won the toss for position and took advantage of the wind and rain. When the kickoff took place, the Americans found a healthy football team and a vigorous storm howling down upon them. It was almost impossible to make a goal in the face of such wind, and the American team was kept constantly on the defensive. In spite of the odds the Canadians were given a hard battle for half an hour. At last Fred Doll sent the sphere skimming through the American goal, scoring a point for the visitors.

"After a rest, one half the allotted time for the game having been consumed, the teams reversed positions and the Canadians faced the wind. The fight was sharp and brief but the Americans forced the inflated sphere nearer and nearer to the Canadian goal, until at last J. Chapman of the Kearny Rangers drove it between the posts, tying the score. Two more points were afterward scored by the Americans through the clever passing of Swarbrick, Swithenby, McGurck, Gray and Cornell. This gave the Americans a lead of two, which the Canadians could not overcome. The visitors rallied toward the close and secured another point, but the score remained at the end of the game in favor of the American team, 3 to 2."[6]

Two days after the game, the *Toronto Mail*'s report on it noted that "In the forward line the Americans showed great improvement over last year, and played a good square game, relying upon sharp passing and heavy rushes."[7]

Again, the American team was well populated by ONT players, six of them this time, Hughes, Holden, McGurck and Jack Swithenby (but not his brother Joe), plus James Howarth and Joe Swarbrick. There were two from New York Pilgrims, F. Cornell and T. Bright; two from Newark Almas, George Wright and John Gray, and one from Kearny Rangers, J. Chapman.

THE YEARS of ONT's domination of the American Football

Association Cup ended with 1887, however. For five seasons thereafter, it was Fall River's show, as Kearny's Massachusetts counterpart began to assert its strength, and the cup did not return to New Jersey until 1895.

When the Fall River East Ends won the AFA Cup in 1891, the *Fall River Herald*, in reporting on this event, noted that "The East End football club may be called the pioneer of 'association' football in the United States. The club was organized in 1880 by admirers of the game, many of them former residents of Lancashire. . . . At first the East Ends were without competitors. Games were played on the south park for a while against any sort of aggregation that could be got together."[8] The place where the East Ends once played, about a half-block off County Street in Fall River, near the intersection of County and Rocliffe, is now occupied by a group of two-story brick apartment buildings. Looming over the area is the granite Stafford Mill, built in 1871, later a garment factory, now the Furniture City outlet store.

In February 1884, some serious competition for the East Ends developed in the form of a team that was originally called the County Street Rovers.[9]

Within less then a year, that new team, by then called the Fall River Rovers, was listed among the entries in the first American Football Association Cup. Whether they actually played any games in that event is unclear, but they certainly played some in the 1887–88 competition, in which they beat Newark Almas, 5–1, in the final. That game was played at Clark Field in Kearny on April 14, 1888, a day that the *Fall River Herald* called the greatest day in the annals of football in Fall River. In its story on April 16, the *Herald* went on to say:

"The news was telegraphed here Saturday night and announced to the patrons of the Academy from the stage. The members of the Bristol county association at once set about planning a reception for the members of the club on their arrival home on the 6:30 train from Providence tonight. All the clubs of the association have been invited to join the procession which will form on County street and march direct to the Ferry street depot. The line will be formed on the arrival of the Providence train and, headed by the Fall River brass band, and march through Ferry, Columbia, South Main, Pleasant, Twelfth, Bedford, Quarry, Pleasant, Thomas and County streets to the Star Music hall, where a supper will be spread, to be followed by a concert and dancing.

"Already the preparations for a rousing reception are being made. On County street, two banners are hung, on one of which is printed "Welcome home, champions of America." The other bears the legend, "You have won credit for yourselves and your town.""[10]

The similarity to municipal celebrations for championship-winning American sports teams in recent years is striking.

The biggest victory for the Fall River Rovers in those years, however, may have come in a "friendly" match in 1887 rather than in the AFA Cup. ONT's reign as AFA Cup champions wasn't over yet. The Clark team was still a few months away from winning its third title, and it had beaten Fall River Rovers in Fall River on Jan. 1, 1887. However, in what might be counted as a passing of the torch, ONT lost on Feb. 22, 1887, Washington's Birthday, when the team from Fall River came to New Jersey, wearing uniforms that called them the Hargreave Manufacturing Company Rovers, another of their early labels. By whatever name, they scored a 3–2 victory over ONT that day, in one of the biggest games ever between a team from Fall River and a team from Kearny.

The next day's *Newark Evening News* described the scene:

"It was a battle of giants, as the victors in yesterday's struggle are famous kickers, and hold the title of 'Champions of New England.' [Actually, they were champions only of Bristol County, but probably were New England's best.] Their well known prestige among the athletes of the Bay State drew a great throng to the grounds, all hoping that the lively young men from Clark's Thread Works would be pushed hard to win. None, with the exception of the delegation from Fall River, desired to witness the defeat of the home players, but the visitors were generously cheered by all on their gallant victory.

"Hundreds of people, both old and young, whose bank accounts would not warrant an outlay of twenty-five cents, viewed the struggle from the Erie Railroad, while scores of enterprising youngsters perched upon sheds and cheered enthusiastically. Shortly before 3 o'clock the Thistle band struck up a spirited air and twenty-two agile men trotted briskly to the ground and arrayed themselves at opposite ends of the field.

"The O.N.T.'s were clad in snug-fitting costumes of bar-striped shirts and stockings, the regulation shoe and curiously shaped caps corresponding with their striped shirts. About one-half the number wore shin guards.

"The Rovers appeared in yellow shirts, across the front of which were the words Hargreave Manufacturing Company Rovers, navy blue trunks, red stockings, shoes and shin guards. They wore no head covering. There were several large men among their number, but on the whole they did not present such a formidable appearance as the muscular O.N.T.'s. The Rovers are a fleet limbed lot, however, and this fact alone saved them from a crushing defeat, for in tackling, they cannot cope with the Jerseymen."[11]

The score was tied, 1–1, at halftime, and ONT took a 2–1 lead in the middle of the second half, but in the waning minutes Fall River pulled ahead, first on what would now be called an own-goal, in the scramble following a penalty kick, and then on what the newspaper called a "beautiful drive" by James Blakely.[12]

The Fall River Rovers were to win even bigger honors later, particularly in 1917, than those they won in the late 1880s, but their number-one legacy to American soccer is not in their biggest victories but as the earliest team to remain a force for more than just a few years. A few other teams in Fall River, New Jersey and St. Louis began earlier, but most of them were gone from the scene well before 1900. The Fall River Rovers didn't disappear from American soccer records until 1922, a tenure of 38 years. In that way did they most signficantly win credit for themselves and their town.

The Fall River Rovers' AFA Cup victories in 1888 and 1889 established Fall River's soccer reputation. The victories by the Fall River Olympics in 1890 and the Fall River East Ends in 1891 and 1892 cemented it. As the *Fall River Herald* said after the 1891 triumph: "Fall River has again been shown to be the capital of the American football world."[13] That may or may not have been true, but Fall River's boosters can't be faulted for saying it.

Perhaps the greatest honors of all in Fall River and Pawtucket soccer before 1900 fell to the players from those cities who were chosen to go on a joint Canadian-American tour of England in 1891. At first, the tour was to have been by just a Canadian team, but then plans were changed, according to Canadian soccer historian Colin Jose. In *Keeping Score,* his history of Canadian soccer, Jose says there was initially a great deal of enthusiam among top Canadian players, but this waned after a disappointing performance against a visiting New England all-star team in June 1891. Some of the Canadian players dropped out of the planned tour, but two of the tour's organizers quickly arranged to have players from the New England team take their places.[14] Eight New England players went on the tour: Dennis Shea, Joseph Buckley, Henry Waring and Robert Bell of Fall River Rovers; James Dalton, Alex Jeffrey and Neil Munro of Pawtucket, and James Whitaker of Fall River Olympic.

The tour was a grueling one. It lasted from Aug. 22, 1891 to Jan. 4, 1892. In that four-and-a-half month stretch, 58 games were played, many of them against top-flight English professional teams. The tour produced 13 victories, 13 ties and 32 defeats,[15] but it was the best exposure to English soccer that any American players had ever had.

DURING THESE YEARS when teams from Kearny and Fall River were faring so well in the AFA Cup, and supplying players for international games and overseas tours, they were forming indispensible cradles for the sport in the United States. It is worthwhile to note, however, that there were other cradles.

The most important of those probably was St. Louis, where the first soccer game to be played was between the Athletic Club and the Mound City Club in 1881. Other teams active in the first year of St. Louis soccer included the Thistles, a Scottish team, and the Hibernians, an Irish team.[16] St. Louis has long been called the first city of American soccer, and that probably is true, considering that it is much larger than Fall River or Kearny. Today, it is struggling to stay among the 50 largest American cities, but in 1900 it was number four, exceeded only by New York, Chicago and Philadelphia. It was a very big city, whereas Fall River was at best a medium-sized one, and Kearny never really more than a town.

In St. Louis, as elsewhere, the strength of soccer in those early decades was aided by immigration, but a great deal of that immigration was from a place where soccer had not taken hold, and wouldn't for another century, Ireland. The first outstanding soccer team to develop in St. Louis, probably the equal of eastern teams, was St. Leo's, which won the St. Louis Soccer League title 10 times in a row between 1905 and 1914. The St. Leo's team grew out of the St. Leo's Sodality, a Catholic parish men's club. St. Leo's was not the only leading team in St. Louis soccer in those days to show the

Catholic church influence, with St. Theresa's, St. Rose's and Christian Brothers College also fielding excellent teams.

An unusual feature of St. Louis soccer, all the way up into the North American Soccer League days of the 1970s, has been the frequent determination of St. Louis soccer authorities to rely on native-born players, rather than the imports who have been heavily used by many successful American soccer teams elsewhere over the years. One of those 1881 teams, the Mound City Club, was composed entirely of American-born players[17] and started a trend that lasted for decades. Indeed, one of the reasons why the St. Louis Stars of the NASL were not particularly successful was their insistence on fielding only American players. When other NASL clubs went overseas for players like Pele, Franz Beckenbauer, George Best and Johan Cruyff, the Stars kept their money home. In the 90 years in between the Mound City Club and the St. Louis Stars, many other St. Louis teams followed this same pattern.

Another place where soccer was developing at the same time was New York City, which is actually just a few miles from Kearny. In this case, however, the giant city was poor relation to its tiny neighbor.

Soccer in New York City in those days relied heavily on British immigrants, but not the sort who were filling the textile mills in Fall River and Kearny. The New York City players were more the upper-crust immigrants, playing in teams with names like Nonpareils and Longfellows, and occasionally facing their American counterparts in games like Old Etonians vs. Yale.

New York City was eventually to become a leading center of American soccer, perhaps *the* leading center. The United States Football Association was founded there in 1913. Teams from New York fared well over the years in the American Soccer League. New York was a prime destination throughout the 20th century for touring European and South American professional teams. But before 1900, while it still has to be called one of the cradles of the sport in America, it was a bit different from the others.

Pennsylvania, especially Philadelphia, was yet another cradle, but it was a little slower to develop. The first Philadelphia team to even make the final of the AFA Cup tournament was Philadelphia Manz in 1896. Before World War I, several excellent Philadelphia teams had developed, most notably Tacony, Disston and Hibernians (the first two of which were actually the same team, under different names in different years).

All of those Philadelphia teams paled beside the accomplishments of the Bethlehem Steel team, which started in local leagues near Bethlehem (about 50 miles north of Philadelphia) around 1910 and turned professional a few years later.[18] Bethlehem Steel had an advantage that was shared by a few textile mill teams, particularly in Kearny, and by teams sponsored by shipyards up and down the east coast, namely that it could offer British soccer players more money than its rivals could by providing employment in the steel mill as well as on the soccer team. This formula helped Bethlehem Steel to win the U.S. Open Cup (then called the National Challenge Cup) four times in a five-year stretch. The Steelers won in 1915, '16, '18 and '19, with their only loss coming in the 1917 final to, of course, a Fall River team, Fall River Rovers. Bethlehem also won the cup in 1926, the AFA Cup in 1914, '16, '17, '18, '19 and '24, and the championship of the original American Soccer League in 1922 (playing as Philadelphia FC in hopes of larger attendances in the larger city) and 1927. Also helping Bethlehem was the fact that one of the leading players of the team in its early, amateur years was Horace Edgar Lewis, who was not just another mill hand but one of the top executives of the company, able to funnel money into the soccer team.

Steel mills in western Pennsylvania provided more of Pennsylvania's early soccer successes. Mills in Braddock and Homestead were particularly successful on the soccer field, although not as successful as teams in later decades from small coalmining towns such as Harmarville and Beadling.

With the possible exception of St. Louis, however, Kearny and Fall River had them all beaten as places for soccer to grow.

IN ENGLAND, the formation of the Football Association in 1863 had been followed 25 years later by the formation of a professional league. In Scotland, the formation of the Scottish F.A. in 1873 had been followed 17 years later by the formation of a professional league. This pattern was followed in other countries, including the United States. Here, however, the process that brought the first attempt to form a professional soccer league in 1894 included a particularly American twist. As with many other attempts to form pro soccer leagues in the United States over the years, a lot of the organizers and financial backers were involved in another sport, and it was never quite clear which sport was really the one that was supposed to benefit from this.

That the American League of Professional Football Clubs was the first professional soccer league in the United States is a true statement. What it tends to obscure is the fact that that league lasted for only three weeks, in October 1894. It took place in October because the baseball season was over. *The Encyclopedia of American Soccer History* explains:

"All six teams in the league were located in the northeast and all were sponsored by National League professional baseball teams. The league itself was an attempt to make some profitable use of baseball stadiums that would have otherwise been empty during the offseason. . . .

"The season ended abruptly, the league's directors having decided to discontinue operations. Low attendance virtually everywhere but Baltimore [which had been accused of importing a group of pro players from England] resulted from a variety of causes, but the scheduling of many of the games on weekday afternoons may have been the main one."[19]

That Kearny and Fall River were not among the league's six teams is not really one of the league's mistakes. Those places did not have the large populations that could be expected to produce the sort of support that this league was looking for, nor did they have National League baseball teams. Still, they did have an audience inclined to soccer, and the organizers of this league did not seem to understand much about that sort of audience, a fact most noticeable in their scheduling of games at a time when factory workers would be unable to attend them.

Within a few months, however, this benighted effort had spawned a second attempt, if on a much smaller scale. The National Association Foot Ball League began its first season in March 1895 with five teams: Brooklyn Wanderers, New Rochelle FC of New Rochelle, N.Y., Kearny Scots of Kearny, N.J., Centerville AC of Bayonne, N.J., and Americus AA of West Hoboken, N.J.[20]

The inauguration of this league marks the first appearance in today's soccer records of the hallowed Kearny Scots, a team most often referred to back then as the Scottish-Americans and sometimes said to represent Kearny and sometimes Newark. The Kearny Scots that have lasted until this day, now playing in an elite New Jersey amateur league, were founded in 1931. Even at that length, they may be the oldest still-surviving soccer team in the United States. With their lineage extended back to the 1890s, they certainly would be. There is no clear connection to this earlier team, which folded in 1919 because so many of its players were in the army, but there is certainly a symbolic connection.

The NAFBL was strictly a New Jersey and New York league, with some Pennsylvania teams joining in around the time of World War I. There were no teams from the Fall River-New Bedford-Pawtucket region, and the Southern New England Soccer League had not been founded yet. The main outlet for New England teams was the American Football Association Cup.

BY THE MIDDLE of the 1890s, the AFA Cup was struggling, and the NAFBL had been born into a difficult world for soccer. The reason was the depression of the 1890s, set off by the Panic of 1893, which was the worst economic downturn that the United States had ever experienced to that time. It may still be the worst, worse even than the far more famous Depression of the 1930s.

The Panic of 1893 resulted from several factors, including drops in the size of government gold reserves backing the United States dollar, overexpansion of American railroads and the collapse of a London bank that was a crucial underwriter of American securities.[21]

"During 1893," says the Museum of American Financial History, "nearly 15,000 companies failed, 500 banks went into receivership, and nearly 30 percent of the country's rail system was financially insolvent. For the next three years, the United States went into deep depression. Strikes intensified throughout the country and personal suffering increased."[22]

The best known of the strikes in that decade were one that began at the Homestead steel mill near Pittsburgh in 1892 and the one at the Pullman railroad car plant near Chicago in 1894, but there also were significant textile strikes in Fall River in 1894 and New Bedford in 1898.

In all, it was not a period designed for sports to flourish, certainly not a sport on the fringes of what little public consciousness of sports there yet was. Soccer's main sports competitors for public attention back then were baseball and college football, but significant inroads into soccer's position in the sporting public's mind were being made by the growing state-by-state legalization of boxing and horse racing. Bicycle racing and bowling also took up amounts of public attention that would be surprising to an American sports fan today.

Mills in Fall River were not as badly hit by the depression of the 1890s as much of American industry, perhaps thanks to a speculative and fortuitious purchase of a large amount of raw cotton in November 1893 by one of the leaders of the Fall River cotton industry, Matthew Chaloner Durfee Borden.[23]

Nevertheless, soccer, hit by the trickle-down effect of the depression, went into something of a hiatus in West Hudson and in southeastern New England in the last years of the 19th century and the first years of the 20th century. It does appear that this hiatus was limited mostly to the eastern areas that were giving themselves exaggerated labels like the "National" league and the "American" association. Soccer activities in growing midwestern centers of the sport such as Chicago and St. Louis seem to have continued about as usual, and leagues that lasted for many years such as the Greater Los Angeles Soccer League and the Associated Cricket Clubs League of Philadelphia were founded in this period. However, the fourth season of the NAFBL, in which Paterson True Blues beat Kearny Scots by only 23 points to 22 in the final standings, was not followed by a fifth season, at least not yet. The 1898 edition of the AFA Cup, won by Arlington AA of Kearny, appeared for a while as though it might be the last.

Over the next few years, soccer in Fall River and Kearny didn't dry up and go away, but it was mostly limited to local games and local leagues, as it had been all along in some other parts of the country. There were various fits and starts at keeping the league and cup competitions going. In 1901, Kearny Scots, Arlington and Paterson True Blues played a three-cornered series that was labelled as being for the American Cup, but wasn't really. In 1902, a league series was begun in New Jersey under the title of the American Association Football League, but nothing much came of it. A team of Fall River players won the soccer championship at the Pan-American Exposition in Buffalo in 1901, beating a Toronto team in the final. For a few seasons afterward, they played under the name

"Pan-Americans" in Fall River area competition and in occasional friendlies against visiting New Jersey teams. Still, it took a visit from an English team in 1905 to really jump start the sport in the eastern United States once again.

The Pilgrims were not the best that English soccer had to offer. They were selected from the leading English amateur clubs,[24] and English soccer was thoroughly professional by 1905. Still, they often overwhelmed the American teams they faced. The places where they played included big cities like New York, Philadelphia and Chicago, but they didn't overlook significant teams from smaller places like Coal City, Ill.; Kearny, and Fall River.

The Pilgrims made two American tours, in 1905 and 1909. A similar team of English amateur players, the Corinthians, toured in several others years. (The Corinthians were past their peak by then, but for a time in the 1880s and '90s they really had been the best in English soccer, often beating the best professional teams by wide scores.)[25] The 1905 Pilgrims played 23 games in the United States and Canada, winning 21 of those. Of the victories, one of the most difficult was a 4–3 triumph over the Fall River Rovers, who had emerged from the hiatus of 1898–1905 still one of the leading American clubs, in Fall River on Oct. 18, 1905. In 1909, when the Pilgrims tour was entirely within the United States and they won 16, lost 2 and tied 4, they played twice in Fall River. A 1–1 tie with a Fall River all-star team on Nov. 10 was followed by a 2–1 loss to the Fall River Rovers three days later. (The Rovers, often at their best against these English teams, had beaten the Corinthians by 3–0 in 1907.) The 1909 tour also included a game against the Scottish-Americans, who were playing their games in Newark rather than Kearny at that point, at Wiedenmeyer's Park.

The Pilgrims won that game on Oct. 10, 1909 by 5–0, not really surprising in view of the fact that the Scots were not the best that the West Hudson area had to offer at that point. In fact, the Scots, except for their run of five consecutive American Soccer League championships from 1937 to 1941, were usually just below the best level.

Unfortunately, while the Pilgrims and Corinthians did meet New England's best in the Fall River Rovers on their tours, they faced neither of the two strongest teams from the West Hudson area in that era. Those were the Clark AA, the successor to ONT as the team sponsored by the Clark Thread Company, and the West

Hudson AA, a team that was formed in 1905 and had hit the ground running when eastern soccer came out of its doldrums.

After that first Pilgrims tour, it was only a matter of months before the American Football Association and the National Association Foot Ball League were reorganized, both in 1906. The 1910 Spalding Guide tells of the rebirth of the AFA.

"In February 1906, a meeting was called by Hal Holden, a well known and popular association foot ball enthusiast of Kearny, to discuss the advisability of reorganizing the American Football Association. The meeting was attended by all the managers of clubs in this section and the reorganization of the Association was immediately effected. . . .

"The following clubs entered the competition for the cup in 1906: True Blues, Paterson Rangers and Celtics of Paterson, West Hudsons, Kearny Stars, Riversides and Caledonians of Kearny, Bronx Rangers and Burns Club of New York, O.N.T. and Scottish-Americans of Newark. The cup was won by the West Hudsons after two great struggles with the True Blues of Paterson."[26]

The NAFBL was restarted just six months after the AFA, at a meeting on Aug. 14, 1906 in Kearny.[27] The league championship was won in the first season back by West Hudson, which had very quickly become the most successful New Jersey team. In that first season of the renewed NAFBL, West Hudson finished atop the nine-team league with 39 points, to 37 for Kearny Scots and 32 for Paterson True Blues.

West Hudson, which was located in Harrison, not Kearny, had been organized in the fall of 1905 in rather informal fashion by a Harrison man, Robert Marshall, after seeing the Caledonians of New York defeat Hollywood Inn of Yonkers, N.Y. in the Metropolitan Cup final. According to the 1911 Spalding Guide, "Mr. Marshall challenged the winners and said he could pick a local team and beat them. . . . The same was done and the game was played with the Caledonians, who had won the championship, and the Hudsons won, 4–1. Then the Hudsons organized into a permanent club and entered into the Metropolitan City League of New York and the New Jersey State League and won the championships of both leagues."[28]

After winning both the AFA Cup and the NAFBL in their first seasons back, West Hudson surrendered each title a year later. Clark

AA, which had changed its name from ONT shortly after rentering the re-formed AFA in 1906, swept to the AFA Cup title in 1907, beating West Hudson, 4–0, in the quarterfinals, Paterson True Blues, 1–0, in the semifinals and Kearny Scots, 4–0, in the final.

The same few teams continued to dominate the AFA Cup in the next two seasons. West Hudson took back the cup in 1908, defeating Paterson True Blues, 3–2, and the True Blues, who hadn't won the cup since 1896, took it in 1909 with a 2–1 victory over Clark AA.

The New England teams had gotten involved in the AFA Cup again in 1908, and in both of those years the Fall River Rovers reached the semifinals. In 1908, they lost a 3–2 semifinal to Paterson True Blues and in 1909, Clark AA put them out, 2–0. The soccer rivalry between the southeastern New England teams and the West Hudson teams was growing, and in late 1909, perhaps inspired by the second Pilgrims tour, an attempt was made to form a league incorporating the best teams of both sections. *The Encyclopedia of American Soccer History* says that the Eastern Professional Soccer League, which would have replaced the NAFBL as the top league in the northeastern United States if it had succeeded, "may have been the first attempt to form a professional soccer league in the United States that was not tied to baseball." The league's six teams were Fall River Rovers, Howard & Bullough of Pawtucket, R.I., West Hudson AA, Newark FC, Philadelphia Hibernians and Philadelphia Thistles. Fall River Rovers were in first place, followed by Howard & Bullough, when the league went out of business in 1910, before completing its first season, defeated more by problems with the weather and scheduling than by attendance.[29]

A few weeks before the league's demise, the *Newark Evening News* had said that the Fall River Rovers "look like sure winners"[30] of the league, high praise for a Fall River team from a New Jersey newspaper.

Ironically, considering the strength of the Fall River Rovers throughout this era, the first New England team since before the hiatus to win the AFA Cup was Howard & Bullough in 1911. The Fall River Rovers were eliminated in the semifinals yet again in 1910, this time by Philadelphia Tacony, 2–1. Then in 1911, Howard & Bullough powered to the title. The team from Pawtucket, sponsored by a company that made machinery for textile mills, defeated West Hudson, 2–1, in the eighth-finals; Paterson True Blues, 1–0, in the quarterfinals; Philadelphia Tacony, 2–1, in the semifinals, and Philadelphia Hiberians, 3–1, in the final.

In 1912, West Hudson came to the fore again, and may have become the first winner of the league-cup double in American soccer. The "double" is a concept borrowed from English soccer, involving winning both the national cup and the championship of the top league in the same season. In recent decades, the English double has become common, with both Manchester United and Arsenal doing it more than once. It wasn't always so, and Tottenham Hotspur's triumph in 1961, when it became the first team in the 20th century to win the English double, is one of the most famous events in English soccer history.

That West Hudson won the cup half of the American double in 1912 is unquestioned. The team from Harrison beat Paterson Rangers, 1–0, in the final after having defeated J&P Coats of Pawtucket, Paterson Wilberforce and Philadelphia Victor in earlier rounds. The league is more problematic. When the first American Soccer League began operations in 1921, there was no question that it was the top league in the United States, despite the fact that it covered a range of only from Philadelphia to Boston, but earlier years are not as clear. In 1912, the National Association Foot Ball League probably was the best league in the United States, but not by a wide margin. In the 1911–12 season, it included six teams from northern New Jersey and two from New York, with West Hudson outdistancing Paterson Wilberforce for the title, 20 points to 16. Leagues in Southern New England, Chicago, St. Louis, Philadelphia and Los Angeles probably were a bit below the level of the NAFBL. The NAFBL does appear to have been the best league in the country, but whether it can be considered so preeminent in American soccer as to constitute the league half of a double is another matter. Still, West Hudson can at least make some claim to have won the double in 1912.

A year later, Paterson True Blues won the AFA Cup, an impressive feat considering that on April 27, 1913, when the True Blues beat Philadelphia Tacony in the final, 2–1, Paterson's silk mills were embroiled in a strike that was one of the bitterest and most debilitating in all of American labor history.

PATERSON'S VICTORY in the AFA Cup was not the biggest thing in American soccer that year, or even that month. On April 5, 1913, in an event that had a profound effect on soccer in both West Hudson and southeastern New England, the United States Football Association (USFA) was formed. This was the first national governing body of the sport in the United States that, unlike the AFA, really was national. It also is the same organization that has continued to this day as the national govering body of soccer in the United States, first as the United States Football Association, then changing its name to the United States Soccer Football Association in 1945 and the United States Soccer Federation in 1974.

The effect in West Hudson was primarily that influence was taken away from that area. The American Football Association had been first and foremost a northern New Jersey organization, and the United States Football Association was not. Kearny was no longer the administrative focal point of American soccer. The effect in southeastern New England was that the teams there quickly understood that the new organization was going to eclipse the old one and redirected their efforts. After 1913, only a few New England teams ever reached the final of the AFA Cup, which finally expired in 1929, partly because not many really tried, having turned their main efforts toward the new National Challenge Cup.

The events that constituted the formation of the United States Football Association began in 1911, when the American Amateur Football Assocation, the forerunner of the USFA, was founded, and were completed in 1914, when the USFA was accepted into membership in FIFA, the world govering body of the sport. Those well-documented events are not really a part of this story of New Jersey and New England, although regional associations from both of those areas were among the founding members of the USFA. While the AFA originally resisted the new organization, and competed hard to gain FIFA membership itself, it eventually joined in.

Where the birth of the USFA does particularly affect this story is through the new competition that was started by the new organization in its first year. Today, that tournament is called the U.S. Open Cup, and the name of Lamar Hunt was added to it in 1999 to honor the man who has been one of the most stalwart backers of leading American professional teams in recent decades. At its inception in the 1913–14 season, and for a number of years afterward, it was called the National Challenge Cup.

The USFA may have had a more national outlook than the AFA, but it didn't have to look beyond the AFA's prime regions to find good fields for the final of its new tournament. The first final of the National Challenge Cup, between two Brooklyn teams on May 16, 1914, was played at the Lonsdale Avenue Ground in Pawtucket, the home field of the J&P Coats team. The third, fourth and fifth finals also were on that field, although the fifth was a draw that had to be replayed in Harrison. Those four finals in Pawtucket drew a combined crowd of 34,000, very good in that day, and the 1919 and 1921 finals in Fall River drew a total of 17,000. Those numbers in relatively small cities, but ones that cared about soccer, must have had the organizers of that 1894 pro league wondering what had looked so good to them about big cities like Washington and Baltimore.

The first years of the National Challenge Cup also saw the emergence of some teams from southeastern New England that had never made much of an impression in the AFA Cup. In 1914, the New Bedford FC reached the semifinals before being eliminated by the eventual winner, Brooklyn Field Club. To this point, soccer in New Bedford had been limited largely to local factory leagues without much outside involvement, even though New Bedford had by now surpassed Fall River as the nation's leading cotton manufacturing center.[31] A year later, J&P Coats made the semifinals. Then it was 1916, and time for the Fall River Rovers to rise again for a last hurrah.

IN 1916, 1917 and 1918, Fall River Rovers played a series of five games that ranked as the most heated intersectional rivalry to that point in American soccer. All five were against the same opponent. Unfortunately for the Rovers, who only got one victory and one tie out of the five games, that opponent was Bethlehem Steel, which had emerged very suddenly as the greatest team that American soccer had yet seen.

The May 7, 1916 final, in Pawtucket, produced a 1–0 victory for Bethlehem, on a penalty kick by one of its greatest forwards, Whitey Fleming. Perhaps more significantly, it also produced the first serious riot in American soccer history. Both events came late in the second half, and both were described in some detail (also with some bias) by the following day's *Bethlehem Globe*, which said:

"The play that helped decide the game came ten minutes from the end of the contest. Just as [Neil] Clarke, the rangy center forward of the Bethlehem team jumped in the air to head a ball toward the

Rover goal, Charlie Burns, the Rovers' left halfback, ducked into Clarke and threw him head-long into the turf. Instantly referee [David] Whyte's whistle sounded for a penalty kick and the Rovers swarmed around Whyte like a lot of wild men, gesticulating and even threatening the referee. 'Sinker' Sullivan, the fiery inside right of the Rovers, persisted in protesting so violently that the hundreds of Fall River rooters in the stands, distinguishable by the yellow cards in their hats, took up the refrain and raised a fearful din of disapproval that continued throughout the remaining ten minutes of play. After cooler heads had prevailed, the Rovers drew back and allowed Fleming, the blond outside left of the Bethlehems team, to make the free kick. [Goalkeeper Jack] Albion pluckily attempted to save the shot, but it whistled by him like a bullet into the net for the goal that won the game.

"The Rovers in the last ten minutes fought like demons for the equalizing score, but they were so angry and excited that they had no semblance of teamwork. Their rough, plunging style of play, however, worked the fans into a frenzy. A few seconds before the time limit, the ball glanced off one Bethlehems player and struck another on the wrist and the Rover fans and players yelled, 'Penalty! Penalty!' Whyte, however, did not see the play and raised his whistle to his mouth to end the game. Even as he did he was stuck in the back by a fan who had been in the lead in the wild rush at the referee. His failure to call what the Rovers thought was a penalty kick for their team seemed the last straw and in an instant Whyte disappeared in the seething mob. The Pawtucket police headed by Lieut. D.A. Ballou drew their clubs and rushed to the assistance of the players who were doing their best to protect the referee, especially [William] Booth who was beaten black and blue. Bottles began to fly and the tumult didn't cease until one of the officers drew his revolver. That cowed the rest into submission and Whyte and the Bethlehem players got off the field into safety."[32]

The Steelers got another victory over the Rovers two weeks later when they beat them, 3–1, in the semifinals of the AFA Cup, which by this point had become a lesser tournament than the National Challenge Cup. But the Fall River team got revenge a year later, when the two met again in the National Challenge Cup final, once again in Pawtucket.

In additional to creating a heated rivalry, these games were beginning to point out a split in the playing styles in American soccer in those days, one that looks a bit ironic when viewed from the 21st century. Bethlehem Steel was bringing in British players, particularly from Scotland, who had been trained in the way that the game was being played there at the time, the "combination" system that blended dribbling and passing to produce a style not unlike the deft, short-passing game of Brazilian soccer in later decades (albeit with less-than-Brazilian skill). Meanwhile, the Fall River players of that era were no longer mostly recent immigrants. It was now 40 years since the runaway growth of Fall River in the 1870s, immigration from England had tailed off, and Fall River players now were largely of a generation that had been raised in America, and played the game in what was becoming the dominant American style of the day, characterized by hard running, long passing and forceful forward movement of the ball.

Today, it is often said that the United States doesn't have a style of soccer uniquely its own. However, *The Encyclopedia of American Soccer History* notes that it once may have. This style was displayed most visibly in some U.S. Open Cup games before 1925 in which teams consisting primarily of imported players faced teams of native-born players. The tendency was for the imported players to play in the short-passing style then popular in Britain, while the native-born players used a more forceful attacking method. As seen from the perspective of decades later, this method often looks like a foreshadowing of the unsubtle style for which British and Irish teams were often heavily criticized in the 1980s and '90s. Ironically, the American teams like Fall River Rovers and Ben Millers of St. Louis that used this style before 1925 were often widely praised for their breaking away from Old World tactics.[33]

This contrast in styles had been seen at least as far back as 1906, when the touring English Corinthians played in Fall River. The *Fall River Herald* said: "The Londoners were very fast, yet they played such a short passing game that they semed to be much slower in movement than the locals. It was exceedingly rare to see a long shot up the field, and whenever the forward line of the Britishers got the ball they seemed to close in and make a compact formation in their attack on the opposing citadel. On the other hand, Fall River played the customary style of game, long kicking, long passing and continuous rushing."[34]

That difference in styles is not directly discussed in the *New York Times* account of the 1917 National Challenge Cup final, which was one of the great games in American soccer history, but it can be inferred, particularly in the fact that the Fall River team seemed to be using what would today be called a defend-and-counterattack strategy. The *Times* account (which included one major error) the day after the May 5, 1917 game stated:

"A rush in the first minute of play and a shot by Sullivan [this is the error, the goalscorer was Thomas Swords] from the 18-yard line gave the Fall River Rovers a victory over Bethlehem and the soccer championship of the United States today. The score was 1 to 0. Bethlehem was constantly on the offensive, but the mighty work of [Jack] Albion, the Rovers' goal, saved his team from defeat. The difference between the two teams on the offense is illustrated by the fact that Albion or his teammates—but chiefly Albion—saved the Rovers about two dozen times [when] it looked as if well directed shots would tally for Bethlehem. [William] Duncan, at goal for Bethlehem, had opportunity for only three or four saves, besides the goal that surprised him and the rest of the Bethlehem team at the start of the game.

"Bethlehem won the toss and elected to have the Rovers kick off. The Rovers drove down hard and Sullivan [actually Swords], right inside forward, made a long driving kick that proved to be the only score of the ninety minutes of play. It was well placed, and the surprise furnished at the start by a team supposed to be the underdog was cheered by the thousands at the game.

"Bethlehem here forced the playing desperately to overcome the initial advantage. In a drive toward the Rovers' goal, a corner was forced, but nothing came of it. Then the visitors [Bethlehem, since the game was played only about 25 miles from Fall River] got loose again and [William] Forest missed a great try by inches. A foul against [Fred] Pepper gave the visitors another chance for a tally, but it came to naught. [William] Booth, right back of the Rovers, cleared a dangerous shot, and Swords was cautioned for a run-in with [Sam] Fletcher. [Thomas] McFarlane stopped a rush by [Jimmy] Easton of Bethlehem and sent the ball spinning toward the Pennsylvanians' goal, in the course of which a foul against [John] Cullerton [of Fall River] gave the Rovers another opportunity, but it was fruitless.

"The Rovers were on the offensive again, but [Jock] Ferguson cleared a great rush by their forwards with a magnificent kick. It was easily the best defensive effort of the game, and showed the great possibility of the Bethlehem game. Sullivan fouled Fletcher near the Bethlehem's goal and a good chance to score was lost. [Billy] Stone [of Fall River] cleared a strong kick by Forest.

"In a scrimmage in front of the Rovers' goal, Forest missed by a foot and [Whitey] Fleming followed this with a hard shot that went just over the bar. Bethlehem was desperate from so many misses and obtained two corners in quick succession without avail.

"Fletcher here contributed a sensational defensive feat by a somersault [something like what today is called a bicycle kick] in stopping Cullerton. [William] Kirkpatrick fouled, being detected holding, but the Rovers missed, and as the interval arrived Bethlehem had two other lost opportunities. One of them was a shot by [James] Campbell from a conceded corner and the other was from a foul against Easton, after which Pepper had a chance.

"The game was mostly in the Rovers' territory throughout the second half also. Bethlehem forced two corners at the start, and after a foul against Sullivan had enabled the Rovers to add to their misses, Bethlehem forced two corners again, but the chief result was a wide shot by Easton over the bar. Swords made a wide shot for the Rovers, and Ferguson [of Bethlehem] cleared from C[harlie] Burns. The Rovers got into the Bethlehem goal once, but couldn't deliver.

"Forest added to the disheartening misses of Bethlehem by taking the ball up and falling in front of the goal, and as the game neared the end the faint hopes for a last successful drive to tie the score died when Campbell was knocked out by the ball hitting him in the stomach. Bethlehem, however, forced one corner from which Fleming made a good drive, but Albion, the Rovers' goal, was on the job."[35]

The *Times* erred on the identity of the goalscorer, but the *Bethlehem Globe* had a good description of the goal that prevented its local team from winning a third straight National Challenge Cup. The Globe said: "The Rovers kicked off and [Francis] Landy passed to Sullivan, who swung the ball over to Swords, who eluded the backs and gave Duncan no chance whatsoever to save."[36]

Was Swords' goal the biggest in American soccer history to that date? Quite possibly. However, for every 100 present-day American soccer fans who know all about Joe Gaetjens' goal against England in 1950 or Paul Caligiuri's goal against Trinidad in 1989, it would be surprising if even one had ever heard of Swords' goal in 1917.

What does probably distinguish this game more than anything else is the defensive effort by Fall River Rovers. To hold a one-goal lead for 89 minutes against a team as powerful as Bethlehem is an astounding feat, although it did owe something to Bethlehem's ineptitude in front of the goal. May 5, 1917 certainly surpasses April 14, 1888 as "the greatest day in the annals of football in Fall River," and it probably still holds that unofficial honor despite the efforts of teams like Fall River Marksmen and Ponta Delgada in subsequent decades.

Thomas Swords occupies a much larger place in the history of Fall River soccer than as just the scorer of that one goal. He ranks behind only superstars Billy Gonsalves, John Souza and Bert Patenaude among the greatest players ever produced by the Spindle City (or the former Spindle City). Swords, who in the course of his career also played for two other leading teams of the day, Philadelphia Hiberians and New Bedford FC, was the captain of that Fall River Rovers team, and also had been the captain of the first United States national team formed by the new U.S. Soccer Federation. That team, called the All-American Soccer Football Club, had made a 1916 tour of Sweden and Norway (neutrals in World War I, as the United States also was at that point). Among the six games on that tour were full internationals (games between the national teams of two countries) against both of those nations. Late in the first half of the game against Sweden in Stockholm on Aug. 20, 1916, Swords put into the Swedish net what the U.S. Soccer Federation and many others consider to have been the first full international goal ever scored by the United States.

Who paid the price for Bethlehem's frustration against the Fall River Rovers? It was West Hudson AA. The team from Harrison had the misfortune to play Bethlehem in the AFA Cup final on May 13, 1917, a week after the Steelers' defeat in the National Challenge Cup final. The score was 7-0, a result that reflected both Bethlehem's strength and fury, and the fact that the New Jersey teams that had been so great around 1910 were getting a little frayed by this point.

Paterson True Blues had folded during the 1914–15 season, forfeiting to Fall River Rovers in the AFA Cup and failing to complete their schedule in the National Association Foot Ball League. Clark AA had been gone for longer than that. (The Clark Thread Company was beginning to cast its eyes southward, although the first move to Georgia had not been made yet.)

Kearny Scots and West Hudson were still holding on. The Scots had won the AFA Cup in 1915, with the 17-year-old Archie Stark scoring the only goal of a victory over Brooklyn Celtic in the final. A year later, the Scots again reached the AFA Cup final, but lost, 3–0, to the wave of the future from the steel mills of Bethlehem, Pa. Both West Hudson and Kearny Scots were becoming regular losers to Bethlehem in both the National Challenge Cup and the AFA Cup. West Hudson gave it a good try in the quarterfinals of the 1914 AFA Cup, forcing three draws before falling, 4–1, on the third replay. It lost to Bethlehem in the National Challenge Cup in both 1916 and 1917, by 1–0 in the 1916 quarterfinals and 2–0 in the 1917 eighth-finals. Then there was the 7–0 humiliation in the 1917 AFA Cup final. Kearny Scots fell to the Steelers by 3–0 in the quarterfinals of the 1915 National Challenge Cup and by the same score in the 1916 AFA Cup final.

The last big victory in this era by a team from the West Hudson section was Kearny Scots' triumph in the 1915 AFA Cup, which may rank as the biggest ever by the first incarnation of that team. The Scots' opponent in the final, Brooklyn Celtic, was not a bad team at all. It reached the final of the National Challenge Cup both that season and the previous one. In the semifinals of the AFA Cup, it had eliminated none other than Bethlehem Steel, 2–1. So Kearny Scots' 1–0 victory in the final on April 18, 1915 in Newark was a significant triumph. In addition to Archie Stark and his brother Tom, that Kearny Scots team included John "Rabbit" Hemingsley, who was to play for the United States against Norway and Sweden the next year (before Archie Stark ever played for the United States) and went on to play five seasons in the original American Soccer League in the following decade.

The *Newark Evening News* chose to write about the game in rhymed verse, in the same whimsical spirit in which it once in that same era celebrated the passage through Newark of a man walking backwards across the country by putting a mirror-image headline over the story. On April 19, 1915, its story about the AFA Cup final began:

"Came Celtics down, from Brooklyn town, on championship intent. The Scottish clan, 'Ameri-can' on winning, too were bent.

"American Cup, soccer prize was up, on old Athletic Field. Three thousand yelled as result was spelled, one, none, the Celtics yield.

"The invaders lean, with haughty mein, on double cup were set said, 'We've got a hunch, we'll beat this bunch and National Cup we'll get [at that point, the Brooklyn team was also still alive in the National Challenge Cup].'

"Then swelled Celts' chests, neath emerald vests. They'd win without ado. But Archie Stark, 'ere it was dark, made them a humble crew."[37]

The story then went on to tell about the game in similar fashion.

The Spalding Guide was less poetic, but more informative. It said:

"After battling to win the old American cup for fifteen years, the Scottish-Americans of Newark at last won this honor, being returned winners of the American trophy and champions of the American Football Association for 1914–1915. Twice previously [in 1907 and 1910] the Scots had reached the final, but were defeated on both occasions, and their followers were beginning to despair of ever seeing the Scots' name engraved on the historical trophy. The Scots surprised everybody by the brand of football and gameness they exhibited. The team that won the cup for the Scots was far from being an old aggregation. It was made up of a bunch of youngsters, backed up by a few seasoned veterans, and the whole working together in perfect harmony brought about the defeat many times of teams admittedly far superior to the Scots.

"The youngsters to gain fame and glory on the Scots team were the Stark brothers, Tom and Archie, Eddie Holt, Bunt Forfar, John Hemingsley, Angus Whiston, John Barry and Joe Knowles [another, George Rogers, was omitted from this list]. The veterans of the team, all of whom helped materially in the Scots success, were Billy Fenwick, Mike Purdie, Mike Toman (captain) and, later, Alex Monteith."[38]

Archie Stark scored the winning goal in the 65th minute of the game. Or, as the *Newark Evening News* put it: "Twenty-five ticks, the minute clicks, the end was drawing nigh. Young Stark was there, where space was clear, and scored as neat as pie."[39]

Before they got to play the final, the Kearny Scots had to overcome some nearby opposition. In the semifinals, they faced West Hudson, just as they had in the eighth-finals of the National Challenge Cup three weeks earlier.

The *Newark Evening News* emphasized the Scots' youth in its account of the National Challenge Cup game on Feb. 21, 1915, in which Archie Stark scored two goals of a 3–1 Scots victory. The newspaper said:

"Although the West Hudsons were favored by a majority of the spectators, the defeat of the Harrison eleven was by no means unexpected. Composed of young players, many of whom have just been graduated from the amateur ranks, the Scots all season long have displayed rare ability. Two weeks ago yesterday the Scots downed the West Hudsons in a league match by the score of 2 to 1. That game was played on a muddy field. Yesterday weather and field were ideal for a battle, and after ninety minutes of the fastest work ever seen in the field the youthful Scots emerged from the fray with the laurels."[40]

The game was played on the West Hudson team's home field in Harrison, part of the site where the Newark Federal League baseball team's stadium was built two years later (today, it is a large paved area at Third and Middlesex streets, near the Harrison PATH railroad station).

Three weeks later, in the AFA Cup semifinal at Clark Field in East Newark (referred to by the newspaper as Clark's Oval), the result was similar. The Scots won, 2–1, with Archie Stark scoring the winning goal early in the second half on a corner kick by Hemingsley. Said the *Newark Evening News:*

"Youth and speed conquered age and experience in this instance. Throughout the greater part of the game the Scots outplayed their rivals. Only for a few minutes in the final half did the victims show any of their old-time form. For a while, it looked as if they would turn defeat into victory or, at least, be able to draw up on even terms with their opponents. The Scots, however, rallied and managed to keep the Hudsons in check."[41]

Within a few more years, both of these two traditional powers were gone. Unlike a lot of other New Jersey and New England teams over the years, they were not victims of economic forces in the textile industry. Both folded during the 1918–19 season, done in by the shortage of players resulting from the draft in World War I. Kearny Scots were to return in 1931. West Hudson never did.

Fall River Rovers still had one more major final, the National Challenge Cup final of 1918 against, yet again, Bethlehem Steel. After the finals of 1916 and 1917, this one and its replay were something of an anticlimax, regardless of the gushing of the writer in the 1918 Spalding Guide who said that the first game "will go down on record as the greatest match ever played in the United States, it being a credit to the players, teams and to the great international sport."[42] That one, in Pawtucket on May 4, 1918, ended on a 2–2 tie, with all four goals being scored in the first half. There were no further dents in the net during the second 45 minutes or the 30 minutes of overtime. The replay in Harrison on May 19 produced perhaps the least heated game these two rivals had ever played. The Rovers had run out of gas. Bethlehem was up by 2–0 at halftime and added a third goal in the second half. The era of the Fall River Rovers was over.

THE EVENTS OF 1884 and 1894–95 were, in a sense, about to repeat themselves. The federation that superceded the American Football Association had been born in 1913. The league that was to supercede both the National Association Foot Ball League and the on-again-off-again Southern New England Soccer League (SNESL) was to be born in 1921. The NAFBL and the SNESL struggled through their last few seasons.

In the last two seasons of the National Association Foot Ball League, the dominant West Hudson area teams of 10 years before, Clark, Scots and West Hudson, all were gone, as were other familiar New Jersey names such as Paterson True Blues, Newark FC and Jersey City AC. There were still two West Hudson teams in the league. Erie AA of Harrison was a promising team that was to become Harrison FC in the inaugural season of the original American Soccer League. Federal Ship of Kearny was sponsored by the Federal Shipyard, a yard that had been opened by U.S. Steel on the Hackensack River side of Kearny in 1917. It was to be one of the primarily builders of ships for the U.S. Navy for the next 30 years and was employing large numbers of Scottish immigrants.

The dominant team of those last years of the NAFBL, however, was Bethlehem. The Steelers had joined the league in the 1917–18 season, when they finished second, and they won the last three NAFBL titles, in 1919, 1920 and 1921.

The Southern New England Soccer League was the only league

in the northeast that, at its best, could have challenged the NAFBL, but it wasn't at its best all the time. It existed for 14 years, from 1907 to 1921, but its not-quite-as-good-as-it-could-have-been status is underscored by the fact that the Fall River Rovers, who were indisputably New England's best team of the time, did not dominate the Southern New England league. They had more important things on which to concentrate their main efforts, other fish to fry, bigger cups to win. New Bedford FC, informally nicknamed the Whalers (a name that seems of have been applied, formally or informally, to New Bedford teams in every sport for the last century at least), won the championship once. The last championship, in the 1920–21 season, was won by the Fore River Shipyard of Quincy, Mass., on the outskirts of Boston.

New Bedford was not a member of the SNESL in its final season. One team that was a member (and had been through most of the league's existence), was to become one of the mainstays of the original American Soccer League. That was J&P Coats, sponsored by the employees association at the Pawtucket thread manufacturer, which was now a division of Coats & Clark, the two former rivals by then having merged. The league also briefly included a New Bedford team that had what has to have been one of the longest names ever in American soccer, the Young Men's Catholic Total Abstinence Society Football Club, known as the Temps (for temperance).

Only one team from the SNESL, J&P Coats, was in the lineup when the American Soccer League began operations in 1921, although there also was a Fall River team. Four teams from the NAFBL were there, Bethlehem, New York FC, Harrison (which had been Erie AA in the NAFBL) and Todd Shipyard of Brooklyn (which had been Robins Dry Dock in the NAFBL).

The West Hudson area's involvement in the top level of American soccer was to be put on hold for the next decade. In contrast, southeastern New England's involvement was to grow even stronger during that decade than it had been before.

III

The Decade of the Original American Soccer League

T HE FIRST AMERICAN SOCCER LEAGUE, which may have been the best soccer league the United States has ever had by the world standards of its day, began operation in the autumn of 1921. It was built around teams in the Middle Atlantic and New England states, and from 1924 to 1930 included teams from four different southeastern New England cities, Fall River, New Bedford, Pawtucket and Providence. The Fall River Marksmen were the ASL's best team over the course of the league's history, having overtaken Bethlehem Steel by the mid-1920s as the outstanding team in American soccer. The rivalry between southeastern Massachusetts neighbors Fall River and New Bedford grew particularly intense during the years when the Fall River Marksmen were battling the New Bedford Whalers in the ASL.

There is a great irony in all of this. The reason why so much of the ASL was focused on southeastern New England was because soccer had been thriving for decades there, a result of immigration drawn before 1900 by the region's burgeoning textile mills. But in the 1920s, at the same time that the ASL was bringing soccer in southeastern New England to perhaps the greatest heights it had ever known, the New England textile industry was in a desperate nosedive.

It is not uncommon today to read descriptions in newspapers or magazines of once great but now improverished American cities. Consider this statement about Fall River from the magazine *The New Republic*:

". . . shortly after the Civil War she had attained such perfection in her chosen field that she was known as the 'Manchester of America,' 'Queen City of the Cotton Industry in the United States.'

"Her scores of mills gave employment to more than half a hundred thousand people [this figure is actually too high] and more than double that number of individuals looked to her busy spindles and looms for their daily bread. Her mills poured millions of dollars into the pockets of families connected with the industry. They produced over 2,000 miles of cotton cloth every day, and they brought from Europe and Canada many thousands of immigrants seeking opportunity and treasure on the golden shores of the Western Hemisphere.

"But having risen to such dizzying heights in the nineteeth century, she was, during the twentieth, to fathom depths of depression such as such she had never known. Today, Fall River is a city of misery, want, unemployment, hunger and hopelessness. The cloud that shadows her seems to have no silver lining, and she lies almost dormant, while stark want stalks her streets. . . ."[1]

That pathetic description is not a look backwards written in 1960 or 1990. It is from 1924, a year when the Fall River Marksmen won both the ASL and National Challenge Cup titles, the league expanded from eight teams to twelve and its teams went on a spending binge to bring top-flight European players, particularly Scottish ones, to America. Eventually, the ASL was brought down by a combination of factors that included the Depression set off by the stock-market crash of 1929, but for a while, in its New England outposts, the league thrived amazingly in the midst of economic and social disaster.

HOW MUCH of the appeal of spectator sports to the average fan is a matter of escapism? Perhaps a lot. In the American Soccer League of the 1920s, there were no two cities in more desperate economic straits than Fall River and New Bedford. There also were no two cities in which teams were followed more rabidly by their fans than Fall River and New Bedford. At least in part, this is a result of the fanatical rivalry, spreading across all sports and all levels, between those two similar cities 15 miles apart on the southeastern coast of Massachusetts. Bill Reynolds talks of it on the high school basketball level in *Fall River Dreams:*

"There is no bigger game on the schedule than New Bedford," Reynolds says, "and there's an unwritten law in Fall River that until you do it against New Bedford, you really haven't done it at all. . . . It's a rivalry that's gone on for generations, the most pronounced in southeastern Massachusetts, one part tradition, one part hate and acrimony."[2]

It may be the most pronounced rivalry in a far wider area than just southeastern Massachusetts, although such things are difficult to measure. Still, it calls to mind American sports rivalries like the Dodgers vs. Giants and European soccer rivalries like Rangers vs. Celtic. When the New Bedford Whalers joined the American Soccer League for its 1924–25 season, this rivalry was crystalized on the soccer field. In his 1998 history of the original ASL, soccer historian Colin Jose states:

"Certain games, such as the bitterly fought local contests between Fall River and New Bedford, always drew in excess of 10,000. Such was the feeling between the two cities, on the soccer field, that New Bedford refused to regard Mark's Stadium, the home of Fall River, as a neutral ground when playing another ASL team in playoff games. Fall River is never neutral, the Whalers claimed; it is hostile territory."[3]

Mark's Stadium was located where it was, a few blocks on the Rhode Island side of the Massachusetts-Rhode Island state line, so that the Marksmen could play their games on Sundays, as ASL teams in New York and New Jersey did, and still charge admission. The Massachusetts blue laws forbade the charging of admission for sports events on Sunday, so games at the New Bedford Whalers' home stadium, Battery Park, were played on Saturday. Another ASL team, Bethlehem Steel, faced problems with the Pennsylvania blue laws, but unlike New Bedford, it didn't have a nearby rival that had found a way to play on Sunday.

By the time of the American Soccer League, the textile mill employment that had once drawn so many English immigrants to southeastern New England barely existed. But in the last decades of the 19th century and the first two decades of the 20th century,

Portuguese-speaking immigration to the United States had risen sharply.[4] Actually, very little of this immigrant group, the one for which southeastern New England was to become most noted, was from Portugal itself. Most were from the Azores or Cape Verde islands. And, as a general rule, most of the Portuguese immigrants in Fall River didn't even come from the same part of the Azores as most of the Portuguese immigrants in New Bedford, a fact that only increased the rivalry between the two cities.

This split is a result of the fact that, as with all immigrant groups in the United States or anywhere, people tended to cluster in the places where other people from their village, county or, in this case, island, had gone before. The first Portuguese-speaking immigrants to the United States had come from the western Azores, and had settled in New Bedford after getting there aboard New Bedford whaling ships in the early 19th century.

The reason for this, as explained by Leo Pap in *The Portuguese-Americans*, has to do with the the fact that Portuguese laws restricted emigration from the Azores, primarily to preserve the sources of military manpower, and the Portuguese government's controls were much stronger in the eastern Azores, which were closer to the mainland of Portugal. In the western Azorean islands like Fayal, Sao Jorge and Flores, Pap says, it was not too difficult for young men to sneak aboard a whaler at night and get away.[5]

This is echoed by Stephan Thernstrom in *The Harvard Encyclopedia of American Ethnic Groups*, who says that "Early Portuguese immigrants were almost all Azorean men from the west-central and western islands of Sao Jorge, Pico, Faial and Flores who signed on to fill out the crews of shorthanded American whaling vessels. . . . They landed, and often settled in, the whaling ports of New Bedford and Edgartown in Massachusetts, Sag Harbor and Cold Spring Harbor on Long Island, N.Y., and Stonington, Conn."[6] New Bedford, of course, was by far the largest of those whaling ports.

In contrast, says Pap, "The Portuguese did not begin to settle in Fall River in any appreciable numbers until about 1890, when they responded to the labor demand of a rapidly expanding cotton industry. The Fall River mills aimed direct recruiting efforts at the most populous Azorean island, Sao Miguel, in the eastern part of the archipelago. As a result, Fall River's Portuguese element assumed a predominantly Sao Miguelian or 'Micaelense' character . . ."[7]

New Bedford's Portuguese-speaking population also involved a racial factor that Fall River's did not. New Bedford was home to a number of immigrants from Cape Verde, another Atlantic island group, but one much farther distant from the mainland of Portugal, off the coast of West Africa. Cape Verde was a Portuguese possession, and immigrants from there spoke the same language as those from the Azores, but they were much darker skinned, and American immigration authorities generally counted them as African rather than Portuguese. The reasons why they had chosen New Bedford rather than Fall River have to do with the fact that the earliest of them had come to America via New Bedford's whaling ships and also with New Bedford's Quaker-inspired reputation for racial tolerance.[8]

THE RIVALRY between Fall River and New Bedford over the years has been a heated one, but in the original ASL it was not really a very even one. Over the length of that league (not counting the 1932–33 season, when the league was collapsing), Fall River teams played New Bedford teams 49 times in either league play or the U.S. Open Cup. (The National Challenge Cup and the U.S. Open Cup are the same thing, and the two names are used interchangeably in this book.) Those games produced 28 victories for Fall River, 11 victories for New Bedford and 10 ties.[9] Actually, the best Fall River soccer teams were better than the best New Bedford teams fairly consistently in every decade from the 1880s to the 1960s. The best competition that Fall River got on the field in the ASL was from Bethlehem Steel, even though the Steelers had faded a bit from the powerhouse of the previous decade. Still, Fall River vs. New Bedford was *the* rivalry.

Sometimes in lists of U.S. Open Cup winners, the Fall River Rovers, winners in 1917 among their many honors since the 1880s, and the Fall River Marksmen of the ASL, winners in 1924, '27, '30 and '31, have been listed as being the same team, usually simply referred to as Fall River FC. This is not true; they were different teams. Fall River Rovers played their last game ever in the U.S. Open Cup on Oct. 15, 1921, three days after the ASL team, named Fall River United in its first season, played its first U.S. Open Cup game. That week, Fall River Rovers ended an era with a 3–0 loss to J&P Coats of Pawtucket, and Fall River United began one with a 5–0 victory over Prospect Hill FC, a minor team.[10] Fall River United was itself eliminated by J&P Coats the next month and wasn't really much of a team by Fall River standards. It finished sixth in the seven-team ASL, winning only five of its 24 games. Then Sam Mark, a native of Fall River and a local sports promoter, stepped in.

Mark spoke more than 50 years later to Frank McGrath, the sports editor of the *Fall River Herald* and a significant figure in Fall River soccer history himself, about his initial involvement with the ASL:

"'At the time, I was operating a semi-professional baseball team and Harold Crook and Dave Pomfret [both later involved with the New Bedford ASL team] were running the old Rovers soccer team at the Athletic Grounds, corner of Bedford Street and Oak Grove Avenue.

"'The American Soccer League was interested in enrolling [actually continuing] a team from Fall River, a soccer hotbed at the time, and I was asked if I'd be interested in financing a franchise. My answer was that I'd be interested if I could get a place for a team to play.'

"Sam went on to say," McGrath continues, "that his efforts to get the Athletic Grounds for a home field were unsuccessful, 'even though I was told that the Rovers were about to fold.' So, he started a search for a possible site and eventually came up with what became known as Mark Stadium, just over the line in Tiverton.

"In those days, Sunday sports were not allowed in Fall River, but it was a different story in Tiverton, and Sam decided that he would probably be more successful as a Sunday team and he went ahead with plans to locate in Tiverton.

"He had talked with the late Tom Cahill, a powerful soccer figure in those early days of the American League [Cahill was secretary of both the league and the USFA at the time], regarding the franchise, obtained Cahill's OK and posted the franchise fee, which was in the neighborhood of $2,000."[11]

Mark's hunch that he could do well as a Sunday team was absolutely correct. The next year, on Sunday, Nov. 18, 1923, the Marksmen drew a crowd of 14,375 at Mark's Stadium for a U.S. Open Cup game against J&P Coats (a 4–0 win). At the time, that was the second largest crowd that had ever seen a soccer game in the United States, behind only the 15,000 at the U.S. Open Cup final in Harrison, N.J., the previous April.

The New Bedford Whalers joined the ASL for the 1924–25 season, when the league expanded from eight teams to twelve. By this time, the Fall River Marksmen had shown signs of becoming a powerhouse to rival what the Fall River Rovers once had been. Before the 1923–24 season, Bethlehem Steel might still have been counted as the strongest team in American soccer, even though it hadn't won the U.S. Open Cup since 1919, that competition having been won since by St. Louis teams and lesser Eastern teams. It had won the inaugural ASL championship, playing as Philadelphia rather than as Bethlehem. In the 1923–24 season, it still featured a number of top players, particularly Scottish brothers Alex and Walter Jackson.

Fall River played Bethlehem four times in that 1923–24 season. Each won twice. The key game came on May 17, 1924, as Bethlehem was trying to overtake Fall River in the standings. Fall River came into that game with 41 points in the standings, to 32 for Bethlehem. The game was played in Bethlehem, and Bethlehem had to win it in order to have any chance of the ASL title. Fall River swept to a 3–0 victory with two goals by forward Harold Brittan, a former Bethlehem player, and one by midfielder Bill McPherson, who was Fall River's first big-name Scottish star and was to play more ASL games over the course of that league's history than any other man. Bethlehem won its last four games down the homestretch, but after May 17, that wasn't enough, and Fall River won the title, 44 points to 40.

Similarly, Fall River had eliminated Bethlehem from the U.S. Open Cup two months earlier. On March 9, 1924, in the Eastern semifinal of that tournament, the Marksmen won, 2–0. Three weeks later in St. Louis, they defeated Vesper Buick of St. Louis, 4–2, to take the cup. There are plenty of arguments that two earlier "doubles," West Hudson's victories in both the AFA Cup and National Association Foot Ball League in 1912 and Bethlehem's victories in both the National Challenge Cup and NAFBL in 1919 are not the real thing. It you accept those arguments, then Fall River Marksmen in May 1924 became the first winner of an American double.

THE DOUBLE was the good news in Fall River that spring, but within a few months, there was news of a different sort. That other news, of course, had to do with cotton. In July 1924, M.C.D. Borden & Sons announced that it planned to move the machinery out of two Fall

River Iron Works mills and transfer that machinery to new mills in Tennessee. The demise of the textile industry in Fall River was a gradual process over a number of years, but this announcement is considered to have been the signal for the beginning of the end.[12]

The seeds of the demise of the Fall River cotton industry actually had been planted years before, and not just in the obsolete machinery and interlocking directorships that hindered the industry. Shortsighted decisions made in the first two decades of the 20th century about the type of cloth to be produced, going for the hot market of the moment, eventually exposed Fall River to southern competition. John Cumbler explains:

"The early textile industry in the South concentrated mostly on coarse cloth and did not compete directly with Fall River.

"Failing to realize this advantage, the city responded to the long and crippling strike of 1904 by switching over to ring spinners [from the more sophisticated 'mule' spinning machinery, which involved more labor costs] and coarser cloth production. Between 1910 and 1914, its industry stagnated, and production and wages fell. The effects of southern competition, coupled with the failure to invest in technological improvements, finally began to be seen in 'Spindle City.'

"In 1915, war demands began to pour into the city. The war market demand was for coarse cotton cloth, and Fall River, along with other New England textile centers, provided it. The war created new peaks in production, employment, and wages. . . .

"The first few years after the war continued to be good years. . . . Production and employment even surpassed the wartime peaks. But the weakness of Fall River's position (and for that matter, that of all the older centers), together with the steady decline of prices in the 1920s, finally caused its decline as a leading textile center in America."[13] By switching away from print cloth, Fall River had sealed its own fate, or at least hastened it.

Despite the textile industry dying all around them, the Fall River Marksmen, over the next few years, continued from success to success. Of the following eight years, there was only one year, 1928, in which the team failed to win either the American Soccer League title or the U.S. Open Cup (they sometimes won both), although in the last two of these years the team, while keeping its personnel largely intact, had moved away from Fall River.

In 1925, the Marksmen won their second consecutive ASL championship in a close race with Bethlehem Steel, against which they had two victories, a loss and a tie that season. Fall River was able to concentrate all of its effort on the league race that season, because the ASL clubs were boycotting the National Challenge Cup. The Fall River-Bethlehem games often fell in mid-season and earlier, rather than the homestretch. In the 1924–25 season, the last of those four games was played on Feb. 21, when Fall River had 12 games left in the 44-game season, and Bethlehem had 13 left. That schedule was a bit longer than it had been before that season. One result was that Bethlehem's Archie Stark, the same Archie Stark who once had starred for Kearny Scots, set a record that still stands today. Stark, who had moved from Scotland to Kearny with his family when he was 12, was now the superstar of Bethlehem Steel, and was the biggest name in American soccer. That season he scored 67 goals for the Steelers, the most that any player has ever scored in one season in a first-division American league (Coming closest are Davie Brown, who lived his entire life in Kearny or East Newark, with 52 for the New York Giants in the 1926–27 ASL season, and Giorgio Chinaglia, with 50 for the New York Cosmos in the 1980 NASL season.)

Fall River Marksmen and Bethlehem Steel each entered the month of May 1925 with 60 points in the standings, but Fall River had four games left to play and Bethlehem only three. On May 2, both teams played scoreless ties, Fall River with Fleischer Yarn in Philadelphia and Bethlehem with Boston Wonder Workers in Bethlehem. The following day, en route home to Fall River, the Marksmen scored a 3–0 victory over Indiana Flooring, a New York City team, to take a lead of 63 points to 61 in the standings. A week later, on May 10, Fall River clinched the title, back home in Fall River, when it scored a 9–0 rout of Fleischer Yarn, while a few miles away in Providence, Bethlehem was beaten by the Providence Clamdiggers, 1–0. That gave the Marksmen a 65–61 lead in the standings, and with each team having only one game left, there was no way that Bethlehem could catch up. The final games of the season, Fall River's 1–1 tie with the Newark Skeeters in New Jersey and Bethlehem's 6–0 win over Philadelphia FC at home, were formalities, although Stark did boost his goalscoring total by five in Bethlehem's runaway. Ironically, none of Fall River's nine goals against Fleischer Yarn on May 10 was scored by the man who was far and away the Marksmen's leading scorer that season, Harold Brittan. Brittan, who had played for Bethlehem Steel in both the NAFBL and the first ASL season, scored 32 goals for Fall River that season, two less than his 1923–24 total.

The Marksmen won the ASL championship again in the 1925–26 season, but this time it wasn't quite as close. Fall River finished with 72 points, again in a 44-game season, and the New Bedford Whalers were second with 61, one of their better seasons. Bethlehem was third with 52 points. The Steelers only played 41 games, but even on a percentage basis, they were well behind Fall River and New Bedford.

New Bedford went into a two-game series with Fall River on April 4 and 11, 1926 trailing the Marksmen by only 57 points to 55. The Whalers had only five games left, to nine left for the Marksmen, but by winning both of those games, they might have been able to tip the scales. Both games ended in scoreless ties, however, and Fall River was able to pull away. Harold Brittan, who by this time was 32 years old, was fading, but the Marksmen had a new scoring hero, Tec White, a forward imported from Scotland. White topped Fall River's goalscorers with 33, but the league's best that year was Andy Stevens of New Bedford with 44, one more than Archie Stark.

In 1927, Fall River failed to collect a fourth consecutive ASL crown, finishing third, 10 points back of the champion, Bethlehem. However, Sam Mark's team recaptured the National Challenge Cup, and eliminated Bethlehem en route to that victory. In the previous decade, Bethlehem and the Fall River Rovers had met three times in the cup final, but with the addition of teams from St. Louis and several other western locations in the early 1920s, the boundary line between the eastern and western halves of the tournament had moved westward. Bethlehem was now in the eastern half of the draw, and thus couldn't meet a Fall River team in the final. It could meet the Marksmen in the eastern semifinal, however, and one of three occasions when it did was on April 24, 1927 in Providence.

Fall River, which had eliminated New Bedford, Fore River of Quincy, Mass., and the Providence Clamdiggers in earlier rounds, won that game, 2–1. The unhappy *Bethlehem Globe* was considerably less than extravagant in its praise for a game in which its local heroes, who had already clinched the ASL title, were deprived of a shot at the double. "The contest proved to be nothing less than a clash of two mediocre teams on the form displayed and lacked the aggressive tactics characteristic of cup competitions," the *Globe* lamented.[14]

Bethlehem had been headed toward halftime with a 1–0 lead, on a goal in the opening minutes, but Fall River scored both of its goals in the final five minutes before the interval. According to the *Globe,* the Bethlehem goalkeeper, Dave Edwards, was at fault on both. The first came after a long free kick by Fall River. Edwards "moved as though to come out and fist it, and then suddenly attempted a retreat, a move which proved costly for he slipped and fell. . . ." Fall River's Dougie Campbell scored easily. With about 30 seconds left before halftime, the ball was crossed from the right "with Edwards watching its flight and apparently making no attempt to handle." Fall River's Dave McEachern was in position to head the ball home.[15]

After getting past Bethlehem Steel, Fall River had it easy in the final, as Bethlehem might have also. A year before, Bethlehem had beaten Ben Millers of St. Louis, 7–2, in the final. This time, Fall River routed Holley Carburetor of Detroit, 7–0. The goals were two by White, two by McEachern, and one each by Campbell, Brittan and Jimmy Kelly.

The next year, 1928, was one of those unusual years when Fall River won neither the ASL title nor the National Challenge Cup. The ASL season was held in two halves in 1927–28, followed by playoffs. The Marksmen did get to the playoffs, by virtue of having finished second in the second half of the season, but they were eliminated by New Bedford in the playoff semifinals on June 10, 1928, a rare big-game triumph for the Whalers over their neighbors. The week before that playoff defeat, the Marksmen had scored a notable success, at least at the box office. Glasgow Rangers of Scotland visited as part of an American tour. The score was 0–0, but the attendance was 15,472, topping the 1923 game against J&P Coats as the most ever at Mark's Stadium. (It did not, however, get Mark's Stadium the record for an American soccer crowd. That record had gone sky high, as 46,000 had seen a game in New York in 1926, between the touring Hakoah team of Vienna and a New York all-star team.) That 1928 ASL title was won by the Boston Wonder Workers, who beat New Bedford, 4–2, in the playoff final. The "Woodsies," named for owner A.G. Wood, included a 19-year-old player who was to earn fame as the greatest soccer talent ever produced by Fall River, Billy Gonsalves.

As if the downturn in the textile industry wasn't enough, 1928 added a fire that further added to Fall River's woes. According to Philip Silvia: "The devastating fire of [Feb. 2–3] 1928, which left Fall River's downtown section in smoldering ruins, ushered in evil days. The city was already teetering on insolvency, beset by an unbalanced budget caused by an irreversible deflation in property values."[16] Appropriately, the fire began on a work site where a textile mill was being torn down. The city was only a few years away from declaring banckruptcy and having its finances taken over by the state of Massachusetts for most of the 1930s. Still, the Fall River Marksmen continued for a few more seasons, actually playing some of their best soccer in their last few years.

The 1928–29 ASL season was the season of the "Soccer War," the battle between the ASL and the USFA for control of the sport in the United States. The war basically was begun by big-business interests within the ASL, particularly Charles Stoneham, who was owner of the New York Giants baseball team and the New York Nationals soccer team. As successful as Sam Mark was, he was not a businessman on that sort of scale. Still, the Marksmen took the ASL side in the Soccer War, which several ASL clubs, most notably Bethlehem Steel, did not. The Soccer War prevented the Marksmen from playing in the National Challenge Cup tournament that season, but they won the 1929 ASL championship handily. The ASL was again divided into two halves. Fall River won both halves, eliminating the necessity for a playoff.

A large part of the reason why Fall River was winning impressively at this time, and would continue to for several years more, was that it was building, through the acquisition of some key players, possibly the most powerful forward line ever seen in American soccer. The very term *forward line* sounds strange today, when teams normally field no more than two forwards. Teams of 75 years ago played an alignment of two fullbacks, three halfbacks and five forwards. The Marksmen had begun building their fabulous forward line a few seasons before, when they acquired Scotsman Tec White. Then, at the beginning of the 1928–29 ASL season, they added Alex McNab, a winger who had played for Boston for the previous four seasons, including the Wonder Workers' championship team of 1928.

The next piece of the puzzle arrived in January 1929 in the person of center forward Bert Patenaude, who had been with J&P Coats of Pawtucket, which was on the verge of folding. Patenaude, who was to star for the United States in the next year's World Cup, was a Fall River kid, the greatest soccer talent ever produced by Fall River's French-Canadian community.

The 1929–30 season was a confused one. It began with the ASL playing without the three teams that had broken away as a result of the Soccer War. Then that dispute was settled in early October 1929, and the schedule was restarted. The Marksmen had acquired Billy Gonsalves from Boston in the summer of 1929, and a few months later Werner Nilsen took the Boston-to-Fall River route on which McNab and Gonsalves had preceded him. By the beginning of 1930, which was to be the greatest year in their history, the Marksman had all the pieces of their forward puzzle in place, McNab, Gonsalves, Patenaude, Nilsen and White.

The Fall River Marksmen of 1930 were probably the best soccer team ever from Fall River. Their most likely rivals for that honor would be the Marksmen of 1924 and 1927, the Fall River Rovers of 1888 and 1917 and Ponta Delgada of 1947. It is impossible to accurately compare teams from different eras. Sports in which performance can be subjectively measured, like track & field, swimming and speed skating, do indicate that athletes have improved markedly over the years. For example, the 4:10 mile by the world record holder of 1930, Paavo Nurmi, would leave him almost 200 yards behind today's best. So, the 1930 Fall River Marksmen might not be able to beat an average team of today. But judgments of who would actually win on the field don't really matter. In comparisons between different years, teams and individual athletes should be judged against the standards of their own era. And by that measure, the 1930 Fall River Marksmen look the best.

It seems appropriate that this was the best Marksmen team, for 1930 was the last full year that the Marksmen were to play in Fall River.

Fall River won the double again in 1930. The league half was easy, or at least looks easy on paper. Once again, the season was divided into two halves, but because of the late start caused by the Soccer War and some other events, it wasn't completed until the fall of 1930. The Marksmen won both halves, with New Bedford second both times. The margin was clear in the first half. The Marksmen finished well ahead on points, despite playing considerably fewer games than New Bedford. They collected 44 points from 27 games, to New Bedford's 35 points from 33 games. The second half was closer, and New Bedford actually had more points, although Fall River's percentage was slightly ahead. Fall River had 34 points from 27 games, for a .630 percentage, while New Bedford had 36 points from 30 games, for a .600 percentage. Over the years, percentage has often been used in American soccer to settle championship races in leagues in which not all teams played the same number of games, those leagues not being as precisely organized as American soccer leagues are today.

The cup was a more difficult battle, primarily because it involved the last two games ever played between Fall River and Bethlehem. The Pennsylvania team folded after this season because the Soccer War had left the Bethlehem Steel vice president who ran the team, Horace Edgar Lewis, disillusioned with the sport and its contentious politics. The Marksmen's first three matchups were with New England teams. They eliminated Lusitania Recreation (better known as Lucy Recs) of Cambridge, Mass., 5–0, on Feb. 2, 1930. Gonsalves had played for Lucy Recs in 1926, the first team he had ever played for outside Fall River, but he failed to score what would have been a symbolic goal in this game. Next, it was New Bedford, and a 5–2 victory on Feb. 22. Fall River products Gonsalves and Patenaude each had two goals against Fall River's eternal rival. The quarterfinals, played in Fall River as the previous two rounds also had been, produced a 5–2 victory on March 2 over Pawtucket Rangers, the team formed after the folding of J&P Coats. Then came Bethlehem Steel, in the eastern semifinals.

The two rivals tied, 1–1, in New York on March 17, 1930. The replay was a week later in New Bedford. *The Encyclopedia of American Soccer History* included an account of the scoring:

"Archie Stark got both of Bethlehem's goals, tying the score at 1–1 and 2–2, but he had no reply to Fall River's third goal. Both of Stark's goals were opportunistic ones, coming when the ball rolled to him out of goalmouth scrambles.

"Billy Gonsalves of Fall River scored the game's first goal in the opening seconds of the second half, after Tec White brought the ball upfield and passed to Gonsalves. Stark quickly tied it, but Dave Priestly put Fall River up by 2–1 with a hard shot through a forest of legs after the ball was centered to him. After Stark had tied the game a second time, Bobby Ballantyne got Fall River's winning goal. Ballantyne dribbled upfield himself, got the ball back after Bethlehem defender Bill Gibson won it away but failed to clear it, and scored with a quick shot to the far post."[17]

As had been the case in 1927, the semifinal against Bethlehem Steel may have been the "real" final. After disposing of the Steelers, the Marksmen didn't have too much trouble with their opponent in the final. That opponent, Bruell Insurance of Cleveland (the team had been called Cleveland Magyars in previous years, but now had a commercial sponsor), went down by 7–2 in the first leg and 2–1 in the second.

Fall River's other achievements for the year had to do with overseas tours. Two Marksmen, Gonsalves and Patenaude, were members of the United States team that played in the first World Cup, in Montevideo, Uruguay, in July 1930. There were 16 players on that squad, but only 11 actually played. The United States fielded the same 11 men in each of its three games, and no substitutions were allowed. Patenaude and Gonsalves both were among those 11, and both increased their international reputations. Patenaude scored four of the United States' seven goals in those three games, and his three against Paraguay on July 17 were the first hat trick in World Cup history.

The Fall River players who didn't go to Uruguay had a big consolation prize. The World Cup team was away from mid-June to early September, playing several games in Brazil on its way home. In the meanwhile, a Fall River team, built around the Marksmen and called the Marksmen, made a six-game tour of Central Europe in August of that year.

The Marksmen players on that tour included a number of the team's biggest stars, such as fullback Charlie McGill, halfback Bill McPherson, and forwards Alex McNab, Werner Nilsen, and Tec White. The 17-man roster also included several New Bedford players, most notably forward Jerry Best (who had played briefly for Fall River in 1929 and was one of the ASL's leading goalscorers for years); several European players picked up along the way, and most dramatically, none other than Archie Stark, formerly of Bethlehem Steel. Stark, Fall River's longtime nemesis, was between teams at that point. The Bethlehem Steel powerhouse had folded a few months before. Stark, along with a number of other former Bethlehem players, ended up playing a few months later for a team called the Newark Americans, who played their games at Clark Field in East Newark.

Stark's presence on the tour caused some controversy, but not because he was playing for a traditional rival. It was because he went on this tour after passing up a place on the United States World Cup team. Stark had a reason, however. When the World Cup team left for Uruguay in June, he said, he was in the midst of getting an automotive business started in Kearny, but he was no longer tied down by August, when Fall River travelled to Europe. Of course, Fall River had a full house of great forwards at that time, but with Gonsalves and Patenaude at the World Cup, Stark and Best fit in nicely. Stark played in Patenaude's center forward spot, and scored four of Fall River's 10 goals on the tour.

On the field, the results of the tour were passable, not bad if you consider that the Marksmen played some of the very best teams of Czechoslovakia, Hungary and Austria. They came home (and started their ASL season a bit late) with two victories, a tie and three defeats. The victories were 3–1 on Aug. 24 in Vienna against FC Austria, and 3–1 again on Aug. 30 in Bratislavia, Czechoslovakia, against a combined team of two leading Slovak clubs, SK Bratislava and Rapid Trnava. Along the way, the Marksmen faced a number of outstanding players, who hadn't been at that year's World Cup because neither Czechoslovakia, Hungary nor Austria entered it. In the first game of the tour, on Aug. 20 in Prague, they played a 2–2 tie with a Slavia Prague team that included five players who were to play for Czechslovakia in the World Cup final in 1934, Frantisek Planicka, Ladislav Zenisek, Frantisek Junek, Frantisek Svoboda and Antonin Puc. The FC Austria team that they beat on Aug. 24 was led by Mathias Sindelar, the halfback who was then nearing the height of the career that made him arguably Austria's greatest player ever, and another member of Austria's 1934 World Cup team, forward Rudi Viertl.

That tie on Aug. 20 was particularly interesting from the standpoint of an American soccer fan. Americans were already getting used to seeing touring European and South American teams come to town described in glowing terms. By the 1950s, it was to become ridiculous, particularly in New York, with nearly every European team that showed up, including some rather ordinary ones, being hailed as fabulous powerhouses. On this occasion, it was the touring Americans who were in that position, arriving in Europe for a game against Slavia that was heralded by the Prague newspapers as being between two superteams, the champions of Czechslovakia and the champions of America. This time, the tourists actually deserved their label, unlike the often overhyped European teams touring the United States. Fall River pulled out the tie on goals by McNab in the 79th minute and Stark in the 80th after having trailed by 2–0.

The other games of the tour, besides the victories and tie, were a 6–0 loss to Weiner AC in Vienna on Aug. 23, a 4–0 loss to Slavia Prague in Prague on Aug. 28, and a 6–2 loss to Ferencvaros in Budapest, Hungary, on Aug. 31.

IN SEPTEMBER 1930, the Marksmen came home to a Fall River that was in a sad state. By the next February, they were gone. The departure of the Marksmen wasn't even a big enough shock to be the lead story in the *Fall River Herald-News*. By 1931, Fall River had become accustomed to seeing local businesses fade into history, and the Marksmen were just one more. The *Herald-News* did put the story on the front page on Feb. 16, 1931, saying: "Fall River is today without a professional soccer club. Yesterday's game at the Stadium between Fall River and the American Soccer League selected eleven marked the final appearance of the local team as a unit representing this city."[18] The story went on to explain that Sam Mark had reached agreement to buy the New York Soccer Club of the ASL, and was combining it with the Marksmen. The combined team would play in New York under the name New York Yankees.

Fall River had been devastated by the dual effects of the Depression and the departure of the textile industry. Says Silvia: "Fall River was an unfortunate foreruner of the national depression by five years. The city became pockmarked by granite tombs. . . . Between 1924 and 1939, twenty-six textile corporations dissolved and seventy-three of 101 mills stopped production. . . . the degeneration ran its full course until the last, straggling mill succumbed to the inevitable and closed its doors in the mid-1960s. Fall River had been the Spindle City. It was no more."[19]

Deepening the downturn in Fall River's case was the fact that a large portion of its population did not have the education that might have made a switch to a different sort of employment easier. Low wages increased the pressure on parents to increase a family's income by pulling children out of school and into the mills at the earliest possible age. According to Cumbler, in 1917, a child labor investigation estimated that over 40 percent of Fall River's children left school in the fourth or fifth grade.[20]

THE MARKSMEN departed in 1931, but Sam Mark did not. He lived the remaining 49 years of his life in and around Fall River, mostly operating small nightclubs. Despite having moved one of Fall River's greatest soccer teams to New York, he was something of a revered local figure. People in Fall River understood that 1931 had been a terrible time that called for terrible actions.

The "Marksmen" won another U.S. Open Cup in 1931, although they did it wearing uniforms that said New York on them rather than Fall River. They did it in rather unusual fashion, taking the third and deciding leg against Chicago Bricklayers, 2–0, despite fielding only 10 men. After a 6–2 victory in the first leg in New York (Patenaude scored five goals), they had gone west for the second leg quite confident, taking only 12 men along. Then Nilsen had to leave after a unexpected tie in the second leg in Chicago and McNab broke a wrist the day before the deciding third leg. McNab, the captain, went onto the field for the pre-game coin toss, then sat down and watched his 10 teammates win the game and the cup. They are listed in the official USSF records as Fall River F.C., rather than New York Yankees, because they had played their first six games of the tournament before their move to New York.

IN NEW BEDFORD, the economic situation of the day was worsened by decisions, which had been made in earlier years, similar to the ones that hastened the demise of the cotton industry in Fall River. As in Fall River, the city's cotton industry turned away from the niche market that it dominated, in New Bedford's case the market for finer grades of cloth, to coarser material, because that market happened to be booming between about 1915 and 1920. But those coarser materials were the same goods that the southern mills made, and by turning to that market instead of their own specialties, the New Bedford mills laid themselves open to southern competition in a way that they would not have had they stuck to their established speciality.

That shortsighted switch made have been even more pronounced in New Bedford than in Fall River, because the machinery in many of New Bedford's mills happened to be particularly adaptable to producing this coarse cloth.

Seymour Wolfbein explains that New Bedford achieved its boom of the war years and those immediately following the war particularly as a result of both the increased manufacturing of automobiles, the tire yarn for which required the very sort of cotton "combing" equipment that New Bedford already had for fine goods production, and an increase in government war orders for various types of coarse cotton.[21]

"In concentrating their production upon the tire yarn and government orders, the cotton textile mills had made a grave decision," Wolfbein says. "The decisions involved concentrating upon spinning rather than weaving, yarn production rather than cloth production, producing the coarser rather than the fine and fancy goods. By getting away from fine goods and turning to more staple products of coarser construction, New Bedford exposed herself to competition from the South, which led in the production of coarse cotton goods. The choice made during the war years laid the groundwork for the depression to come."[22]

LIKE THE FALL RIVER MARKSMEN, the New Bedford Whalers played through years of economic upheaval. But New Bedford didn't fare nearly as spectacularly as Fall River on the fields of the American Soccer League. The Whalers never won a league championship, although they did come very close in 1928.

They qualified for the 1928 playoffs by winning the second half of the 1927–28 split season. In the semifinals, they eliminated Fall River, something that may have felt as good to the New Bedford players as winning the championship. On June 9, 1928, the Whalers beat the Marksmen, 3–1, in the first leg in New Bedford. Sam Chedgzoy, Bill Paterson and Walter Aspden scored the goals. A day later, the Marksmen won, 1–0, in Fall River, but the Whalers had the victory on aggregate goals.

The championship was not to be, however. On June 16 in New Bedford, the Boston Wonder Workers beat the Whalers, 4–2, for their only ASL title. The Boston team that day included several players who were to become Fall River stars in subsequent years, McNab, Gonsalves and Nilsen.

New Bedford did get a U.S. Open Cup victory in 1932, but the team that accomplished that was largely the Marksmen, as a result of yet more maneuverings that were part of the death throes of this original ASL.

Sam Mark had discovered that his team drew no better in New York than it had in Fall River. New York was not affected by the departure of the cotton industry the way Fall River was, but by 1931, the Depression was in full bloom. So, Mark moved his team again, this time to New Bedford, where, naturally, they took the name Whalers.

When these New Bedford Whalers played Stix, Baer & Fuller of St. Louis for the U.S. Open Cup in the spring of 1932, their lineup was dominated by former Marksmen players. Four of that great forward line were there. The only missing man was Bert Patenaude, and he had been replaced by Tom Florie, the captain of the 1930 United States World Cup team. Florie, who may be the greatest soccer player ever to come out of Harrison, N.J., was a longtime star of Providence and New Bedford ASL teams.

New Bedford won the cup by following a 3–3 tie on March 27, 1932, with a 5–2 victory in the replay on April 3. Both games were played in St. Louis. Werner Nilsen, Billy Gonsalves and Florie scored in both games. Tec White and Bill McPherson had the odd goals.

James Robinson noted in his St. Louis soccer history that Sam Mark didn't seem to have lost his financial touch, despite the woes of the previous few years. Wrote Robinson:

"When each Stix player received $26.50 as his share of the gate receipts [after the March 27 game], the team threatened not to play the following Sunday unless new financial arrangements were made. Sam Mark, the New Bedford business manager, complained that there were too many 'country cards' [free passes]. The Stix players suggested that Mr. Mark supervise the business details on the following Sunday, and Mr. Winston E. Barker, president of the Saint Louis Soccer League and a United States Football Association official, approved the arrangement.

"The large crowd convinced the New Bedford team of the wisdom of having the playoff games in Saint Louis, rather than at some other site, even though the Whalers were the 'home' team. So the deciding game was played in Saint Louis on April 3, 1932. In this game, the New Bedford team defeated the Stix eleven, 5–2, for the national championship before 7,371 fans, who paid $6,626.50, at Sportsmen's Park."[23]

A few months before, that New Bedford team had come close to winning the 1931 ASL championship. The championship was decided in a playoff between winners of the spring 1931 championship, the New York Giants, and the fall championship, captured by the New Bedford Whalers after their move from New York in the summer of 1931. The Whalers, most of whom had been Fall River Marksmen less than a year before, won the first the game, 8–3, in New Bedford. Five goals would seem quite a comfortable margin to take into the away game, which was played in New York, but the New York team, which included former Marksman Bert Patenaude, won by 6–0 for a 9–8 aggregate victory. Four of those nine goals were scored by Patenaude.

That may have been a disappointment, but the 1932 victory in St. Louis probably stands as the high point in the history of New Bedford soccer. Even that milestone, however, owed something to Fall River.

PAWTUCKET also was hit by the downturn in the New England textile business, but it wasn't a city devoted to a single industry the way that Fall River and New Bedford were. By the 1930s, Pawtucket was struggling, but that was mostly a result of the Depression, unlike similar troubles in cities like Fall River and New Bedford that had been disaster areas long before the stock market crash of October 1929.

Still, a crucial barometer of the effect that the textile downturn did have on Pawtucket was that the J&P Coats soccer team was disbanded on March 23, 1929, well into New England's textile depression but before the start of the national Depression.

J&P Coats had been sponsoring soccer teams for at least two decades, and the company's effect on Pawtucket soccer had gone back even farther. The Scottish immigration that it drew to Pawtucket had been a large factor in the prominence of Pawtucket teams in the 1890s. Technically, the J&P Coats team of the American

Soccer League was not sponsored directly by the company, but rather by its employees association. That employees assocation seems to have been rather well treated by the company, however. Gary Kulik notes that "In 1921 [which was the year the ASL began], a brick recreation building was erected overlooking Coats' athletic field. The building contained a restaurant capable of seating 2,000, an entertainment hall, bowling alleys, pool tables, and baths. Though the field is now [in 1979] a parking lot, the recreation building survives as a discount department store on Lonsdale Avenue."[24]

Coats, known as the Threadmen, won one American Soccer League championship, in the ASL's second season, 1922–23. Fall River was not then yet much of a factor, but Bethlehem Steel certainly was. Coats narrowly outdistanced the Steelers in the standings, 44 points to 42, with the results turning on the outcome of games that each played against the Paterson Silk Sox in the last month of the season. On May 26, Bethlehem won a game by forfeit from Coats, tying the standings at 42 points apiece. That was Bethlehem's last game of the season, and it could have taken the lead that day had it done better in its next-to-last game, in Paterson on May 6. The Steelers lost to the Silk Sox that day, 3–2. Coats had one game left, in Paterson on June 3, and won it, 2–0, to take the title.

The J&P Coats team that season was led by two of the biggest stars of Bethlehem's powerhouse of a few years before, Whitey Fleming and Jock Ferguson. Fleming was Coats' leading goalscorer that season and Ferguson, who subsequently returned to Bethlehem, anchored the defense, just as he had in Bethlehem's glory years.

For the remainder of its time in the ASL, however, Coats languished toward the bottom of the standings. The team that was formed in 1929 to replace it, Pawtucket Rangers, fared a little better. Pawtucket Rangers made the final of the U.S. Open Cup in 1934 and 1935, losing to Stix, Baer & Fuller of St. Louis both times, and then won the cup in 1941.

Providence teams didn't fare nearly as well in the ASL, despite having some good players like Tom Florie and Andy Auld (both members of the 1930 United States World Cup team) and Joe Kennaway. The Clamdiggers joined the ASL at the start of the 1924–25 season when the league had its biggest expansion, and stayed in it through 1930.

Most of Providence's ASL seasons were mediocre, but it did have one good one, 1928–29, after the team's name had been changed to the Gold Bugs. The Fall River Marksmen won the ASL title that season, taking both halves of a split season and thus collecting the trophy without a playoff. Providence, which was used to finishing somewhere between fifth and eighth in the ASL standings, came very close to winning the second half, which would have forced a playoff for the championship. The Gold Bugs came into the last day of the season, April 21, 1929, just a point behind Fall River, 27-to-26. They played Fall River that day, in Tiverton, and a victory would have boosted them past the Marksmen to the second-half title, but Fall River managed to get a 2–2 tie and the championship.

Providence got a bit of redemption a month later. That was the season of the Soccer War, and one of the features of the struggle was that the ASL teams, which weren't playing in the U.S. Open Cup, revived the old American Cup, or at least held a tournament they called the American Cup. In the final, on May 20 at the Polo Grounds in New York, Providence beat the New York Nationals, 4–2. Three of the Gold Bugs' goals came from Bill Paterson, who had been their leading scorer in the ASL season with 33 goals.

THE ORIGINAL American Soccer League flourished in southeastern New England, despite the downturn of the textile industry. The effects of that downturn were not as severe in New Jersey, because thread and silk were not in direct competition with the southern mills, but while there were several New Jersey teams in the ASL, none of them ever made a big impression.

The longest lasting was the Newark Skeeters, owned by Tom Adams, who had once been manager of the West Hudson AA team. The Skeeters played five seasons in the ASL, and never finished higher than eighth. They were among three teams, along with Bethlehem Steel and the New York Giants, who quit the ASL during the Soccer War, siding with the USFA, but they never returned.

The Skeeters produced one really outstanding player, goalkeeper Jimmy Douglas. Douglas, who was born in East Newark and over the course of his ASL career played for eight different teams, was the United States' goalkeeper at both the 1924 Olympic Games and the 1930 World Cup. He played for Newark in the 1923–24 and 1924–25 seasons.

Harrison SC played in only the first two seasons of the ASL, without notable success. It was, however, a first ASL stop for two of the greatest players that that league produced, Tom Florie, born in Harrison, and Davie Brown, born in Kearny.

Paterson Silk Sox, a successor to the True Blues of earlier decades, did a bit better, but not in the league itself. In their only ASL season, 1922–23, they finished fifth out of eight teams. But in that same season, they won the U.S. Open Cup. They played a 2–2 tie with the defending champion, Scullin Steel of St. Louis, in the final in Harrison. Scullin, more than 1,000 miles from home and suffering injuries, was unable to field a team for the replay and forfeited the title to Paterson. A few years before the start of the ASL, in 1919, Paterson had reached the finals of both the U.S. Open Cup and the American Cup. Unfortunately for Paterson, its opponent in both was Bethlehem Steel. The score in both was the same, 2–0 for the Pennsylvania team.

Still, despite the unsteadiness of these steps, there were some activities going on in the West Hudson area that would lead to soccer success in future years. The most important of these had to do with yet more immigration from Scotland.

Scottish immigration to the United States, which often meant Scottish immigration to Kearny, surged in the 1920s. In Kearny, this was largely a result of two factors, changes in the immigration laws that favored British immigrants and employment opportunities offered not just by the traditional employers of Scots in Kearny such as Clark and Nairn, but also by new business concerns such as the Federal Shipyard and a Western Electric plant.

The same laws that were restricting Portuguese immigration to Fall River and New Bedford were advancing Scottish immigration to Kearny. Those laws were a result of the way that, by the late 1800s, anti-immigration forces had gained strength in the United States. Immigration historian Oscar Handlin wrote:

"Immigration legislation in the nineteenth century had simply aimed to regulate the conditions of entry and to exclude obviously unfit applicants such as lunatics, polygamists, anarchists, the diseased, and persons likely to become a public charge. But the restrictionists sought a different kind of control and turned first to the device of a literacy test, which they assumed would be a reliable measure of the potentiality for citizenship. Congress three times yielded to such demands, in 1896, 1913 and 1915, only to see the bills vetoed by Presidents Cleveland, Taft and Wilson, who objected to radical departure from American policy."[25]

Handlin says the the literacy test that finally was enacted in 1917, over Wilson's veto, did not have the effect desired by the anti-immigrationists, who sought further measures, and got them:

"Three laws passed in 1921, 1924 and 1929 established a new pattern. These measures set an absolute limit of 150,000 annually on all immigration other than that from the Western Hemisphere. The total was, moreover, divided into quotas assigned by a complicated formula to each nationality in accordance with its presumed contribution to the original American stock. Countries of the old immigration, like Britain, Germany and Ireland, received high quotas; those of the new, like Italy, Poland and Greece [and Portugal], received very low ones."[26]

One of the results, says Stephen Thernstrom in *The Harvard Encyclopedia of American Ethnic Groups*, was an upturn in Scottish immigration to the United States:

"Whereas only 78,357 Scots settled in the United States between 1911 and 1920, 159,781 immigrated between 1921 and 1930.

"Therefore the number of people of Scottish birth in the United States continued to rise: 233,473 in 1900, 261,034 in 1910, 254,567 in 1920, and a peak of 354,323 in 1930."[27]

One of those immigrants between 1911 and 1920 made his mark on Kearny soccer more firmly than any other man ever has. The West Hudson area may not have contributed much in the way of teams to the original American Soccer League, but it contributed a lot in the way of individuals, such as Davie Brown, Tom Florie, Jimmy Douglas and, first and foremost, Archie Stark.

Stark, who came to the United States from Scotland with his parents in 1912, was one of the three greatest players in American soccer before World War II, along with Billy Gonsalves and Alex McNab. He set records that still stand for the most goals scored in American first-division play, with 253, and the most in a single season, with 67.

Stark also demonstrated that soccer was not a way to get rich, at least not for an American. *The Encyclopedia of American Soccer History* notes that Stark's 67 goals for Bethlehem Steel in the 1924–25 season "won him a raise to $75 a week, the highest in American soccer at the time."[28]

In addition to the goalscoring records that he set with Bethlehem

Steel, Stark set a mark that has been tied several times but never broken when he scored four goals in one game for the United States national team against Canada in 1926.

Stark had begun his career with New Jersey teams like Kearny Scots, Babcock & Wilcox of Bayonne, Erie AA and Paterson FC. He broke into the ASL with New York FC in the 1921–22 season, and played his first three ASL seasons with that team before being transferred to Bethlehem Steel, where he enjoyed his greatest success (including three five-goal games in league play). He returned to Kearny at the end of his career, playing for Kearny Irish in the restructured ASL, and then operated a tavern on Kearny Avenue, the main street through the middle of town, for decades. Unlike some other prominent players, Stark wasn't born in Kearny, but he is its most famous soccer son.

FALL RIVER had its equivalent of Archie Stark, a decade younger than the Kearny idol, and he was the exception to a rule. Although southeastern New England was well populated with Portuguese-speaking immigrants by the 1920s, very few of them found their way onto the region's American Soccer League teams, although there were plenty of active Portuguese teams in Fall River amateur ranks. Billy Gonsalves most assuredly did become a professional, however, and remained one from the 1920s to the 1940s.

Adelino Gonsalves, who picked up the nickname "Billy" early in his soccer career, was born in Portsmouth, R.I., not far from Fall River, in 1908, the son of recent immigrants from the Portuguese island of Madeira. He grew up in Fall River, but after he left there in his late teens, he became a soccer nomad. He played for teams (in chronological order) in Cambridge, Mass.; Boston; Fall River; New York; New Bedford; St. Louis; Chicago; White Plains, N.Y.; Kearny and Brooklyn.

Perhaps Gonsalves' most famous feat was to have been on teams that won the U.S. Open Cup on eight occasions, and to have played in the final 11 times. He won with the Fall River Marksmen in 1930 and 1931, New Bedford in 1932, Stix, Baer & Fuller of St. Louis in 1933 and 1934 and Central Breweries of St. Louis in 1935. He then was on the losing side with St. Louis Shamrocks in 1936 and 1937, and Manhattan Beer of Chicago in 1939, before winning two more times with Brooklyn Hispano in 1943 and 1944.

Gonsalves was an inside right, mentored in his soccer skills by Alex McNab, the outside right with whom he was paired for many years in Boston, Fall River, New York, New Bedford and St. Louis. He was a big man for a soccer player, 6-foot-2 and over 200 pounds, and perhaps his greatest attribute on the field was his cannon of a shot.

A few days after Gonsalves' death in 1977, Dent McSkimming, a former St. Louis sportswriter who was once the dean of American soccer reporters, was quoted concerning Gonsalves' shot by the *Fall River Herald-News.* "I don't remember a single player anywhere whose shooting was so powerful," McSkimming said. "It tended to overshadow his uncanny ability to tip a header out of the goalie's reach. And his magic in hiding the ball and dribbling out of a tight spot was sensational."[29]

A few years earlier, McSkimming praised Gonsalves' all-around ability to Bob Broeg, the sports editor of the *St. Louis Post-Dispatch,* for which he had once worked. This time, McSkimming said:

"I've always regarded Gonsalves as the closest thing we saw to the ideal, complete player. I recall him as without equal in American soccer, and we had plenty of chance to compare him with world-leading players who opposed him.

"As a reporter, I always asked the foreign players the inevitable question—and in total they agreed that Gonsalves would win a place and be a star on any team in the world."[30]

Gonsalves played for the United States in both the 1930 and 1934 World Cups, playing every minute of the four games that the United States played in those World Cups in Uruguay and Italy. He supposedly was offered professional contracts in Brazil in 1930 (where the United States played en route home) and Italy in 1934 but turned them down. His size has been said to have been the number-one factor in causing the French team at the 1930 World Cup to label the Americans "the shotputters."[31]

IN THE WEST HUDSON AREA, amateur soccer fared no better during the era of the original American Soccer League than did the professionals. In southeastern New England, however, while the pros were thriving, so were the amateurs, which frequently meant Portuguese players.

The National Amateur Cup was founded by the USFA in 1924, to create an outlet for the amateurs who were regularly getting swamped by the pros in the National Challenge Cup. In the first 25 years of the National Amateur Cup, ending with the last of Ponta Delgada's three straight victories in 1948, teams from Fall River or New Bedford were finalists 14 times. Only the Pittsburgh area had a comparable record in amateur soccer in those years.

The first of those 14 finalists were the New Bedford Defenders in 1926, a group of players from the South End of New Bedford who started small but grew to national stature. Unlike the National Challenge Cup victory of the New Bedford Whalers in 1932, this was a home-grown triumph. Arnie Oliver, the leader of that Defenders team and four years later a member of the United States squad at the World Cup, talked to the *New Bedford Standard-Times* 30 years later about the beginnings of the Defenders and that cup effort.

"'The Defenders were organized by a bunch of us fellows around Brock Avenue and David Street,' Oliver reminisced. 'Our first clubrooms were in a store in that neighborhood which has since been torn down. We paid 10 cents a week in dues just to keep things going and when the National Amateur Cup competition came around the $25 entry fee seemed like a fortune.'"[32]

That was 1925, and the Defenders didn't get far in the cup that year. Still, they put up the $25 again the following season, this time with better results.

En route to the 1926 final, they defeated first two Boston teams and then two New York teams, the Imperial FC and the Brooklyn Boroughs. As the Defenders moved through the competition, a Soccer Fund Committee was formed in New Bedford and raised the money to pay for the Defenders' trip to Cleveland for the final.[33] Raising money for amateur soccer in New Bedford in 1926 must have been no easy task.

That final was against the Heidelberg team from near Pittsburgh, and New Bedford sources call Heidelberg a clear favorite, a judgement based largely on the great size and speed of its players. The *New Bedford Standard-Times'* 30-years-later account of the game makes it sound a bit like the 1917 Bethlehem-Fall River Rovers game, dominated by the losing team. The newspaper says:

"Heidelberg pressed practically the entire match, with the New Bedford booters making only a few sorties deep into enemy territory.

"Only the great stops by goalie [Dick] Heap and the yeoman fullback work of [Bob] Seddon, plus timely tightened defenses from all of the other Defenders warded off the continued charges."[34]

The difference between this game and the 1917 one was that this time the winning goal of the 1–0 contest was scored at the very end, rather than the very beginning. Walter Aspden, who later went on the Fall River European tour of 1930, scored it for New Bedford.

Another New Bedford team, LaFlamme Cobblers, reached the final a year later. Heidelberg was back again, and this time won, 3–0. A third New Bedford team, Black Cats, was a finalist in 1931, losing a two-game series to Akron Goodyear.

One of the most impressive things about Fall River amateur soccer in that era was the way that the talent was spread around. By 1942, Fall River teams had made the National Amateur Cup final eight times, but no team had done it more than once. This was not the work of one or two powerhouse teams.

The first Fall River team to get the title was Powers Hudson-Essex, sponsored by an automobile dealership (Powers) that sold Hudson-Essex cars. They shared the title with a Chicago team in 1928. Who was buying cars in Fall River in 1928 is unknown.

Fall River amateur teams in that era seem to have been a mixture of teams with commercial sponsors and teams built around ethnic organizations or churches. That has been the general trend in American soccer over the years, and the ethnic organizations have tended to stay in the game far longer than the commercial sponsors, who came and went. One of the best examples of the latter trend is a St. Louis team that reached the National Challenge Cup final in six consecutive years in the 1930s. The first three years, it was Stix, Baer & Fuller, then Central Breweries for a year and then Shamrocks for two years, but it was all the same team, and was the same team once again as Southside Radio in a seventh year.

Nothing that extreme ever happened in Fall River. But it was true there as anywhere that an Italian church or a Portuguese club was likely to remain involved in the game longer than a tavern or an auto dealership.

Some ethnic separation in Fall River can be seen in the makeup of the teams. The Holy Cross team, one of the leading church-sponsored teams in Fall River in the 1930s, was largely Polish. Another, St. Michael's (the 1939 National Amateur Cup champion) was largely Portuguese, not unsuprisingly, since Sao Miguel is the largest of the eastern Azores.

When amateur soccer in Fall River really did start to become dominated by a single powerhouse was with the rise of Ponta Delgada, which won its first National Amateur Cup in 1938. Before that, Fall River Raffie's, named for the tavern owner who organized the team, won the cup in 1930, beating Gallatin of Western Pennsylvania in the final. Fall River Santo Christo, sponsored by a Portuguese church, was the runnerup in 1932, as was Fall River All-American in 1935.

WHEN PONTA DELGADA came to the fore in the late 1930s, it signaled the start of a new great era, possibly the last great era, in Fall River soccer. In the meanwhile, Kearny had been getting its turn again, in a new version of the American Soccer League.

B. McPherson · E. Tate · F. Kerr · A. Lorimer · H. Brittan

H. McGowan · T. Croft · S. Mark · T. Reeside · B. Fryer

Sam's Marksmen, Fall River Soccer Football Team. 1924 – 1925.

A. Kemp · F. Morley · © Schofield, 1925 · D. Campbell · C. Albion

Courtesy of the National Soccer Hall of Fame

The 1924-25 team was the second of many Fall River Marksmen squads to win American Soccer League titles. Owner Sam Mark, who founded the team in 1922, is in the center.

Archie Stark

Courtesy of the National Soccer Hall of Fame

Bert Patenaude

Courtesy of the National Soccer Hall of Fame

Billy Gonsalves

Courtesy of the National Soccer Hall of Fame

Jimmy Douglas

Courtesy of the National Soccer Hall of Fame

ONT ("Our New Thread") of Kearny can be called the first champion of American soccer, as a result of its victories in the American Football Association Cup in 1885, 1886 and 1887. This 1887 team beat the Kearny Rangers, 3-2, in the AFA Cup final.

Courtesy of the National Soccer Hall of Fame

Tom Florie

Courtesy of the National Soccer Hall of Fame

John Souza

Courtesy of the National Soccer Hall of Fame

Tony Meola

Courtesy of the U.S. Soccer Federation

John Harkes

Courtesy of the U.S. Soccer Federation

Tab Ramos

Courtesy of the U.S. Soccer Federation

Above, the former Bourne Mill looms over the empty field in North Tiverton, R.I., across the state line from Fall River, where Mark's Stadium once stood and both the Marksmen and Ponta Delgada played.

Below, in an area that now is a parking lot in East Newark, N.J., the United States played Canada in 1885 and 1886 on Clark Field, in the shadow of the Mile End Spool Cotton Mill.

IV

Scots and
Pontas

I N THE LAST DECADE, American soccer has seen what is really a rep-
etition of events that first took place 70 years ago. In the current
instance, Major League Soccer has emerged as a scaled-back version of the North American Soccer League. In the early 2000s, MLS
was still losing money, but perhaps it had begun to see the light at
the end of the tunnel. A large part of MLS's hopes for success, since
its off-the-field beginnings in 1993, had been pinned on avoiding the
overspending that has often been blamed for the demise of the
NASL.

Similarly, in 1933, a scaled-back version of the original American
Soccer League emerged. Like MLS, this second ASL was dedicated
to avoiding the financial excesses of its predecessor.

In 1933, the United States was in about the deepest of the
Depression. In southeastern New England, it may have been even
worse, because the departure of the textile industry for its new
home in the South added to the region's troubles. In the West
Hudson area of New Jersey, it wasn't quite as bad as that. Helped by
the more financially conservative atmosphere of this new ASL, the
1930s saw a rebirth in that section of professional soccer, or at least
semipro, for that's what this new ASL was.

The first edition of the annual "Bill Graham Guide," published
in 1948, contains an account of the founding of the new ASL. That

account is often confusing and misleading, but occasionally illuminating. Concerning the Kearny teams, it states:

"At this time [1932], Bill Grant came forward with a proposal to place a team in Newark. A franchise was granted and the team played at Clark's Field in East Newark. Soon, after many difficulties, he withdrew.

"This effort had not been without effect, for it gave ambitions to the Irish-American A.C. of Kearny. James Gaven was the spearhead in the next two seasons. When admitted to the league, the team was without uniforms, but that did not daunt Gaven and his loyal supporters. A house-to-house raffle provided the necessary funds.

"The Scots-Americans of the same city followed in short order and from such humble beginnings, the Irish out of a corner store and the Scots from a top floor apartment, now own their own clubhouses and have bank balances."[1]

That top-floor apartment was on Devon Street in Kearny, and it was there that the foundation of this new American Soccer League had been laid in 1931 with the establishment of the Scots-American Club by 13 members of the Clan Forbes soccer team from the New Jersey State League. Those 13 men were Alex Campbell, Bill Chalmers, Matt Turner, Dave Irwin, Peter Flynn, Jimmy Boyle, Bill Branks, William Milne, Bill Gillespie, Andy Spears, Peter Gray, George Haldane and Matt Dunlop.[2] They were the people who gave new life to the team that had foundered in 1919 but now was reborn and was to advance into the 21st century as probably the oldest soccer team in the United States. The year 1931 was a pivotal one for Kearny in another way. In that year the Clark Thread Company, which had come to New Jersey seven decades before, began leaving, opening a mill in Clarkdale, Ga.[3]

The main body of this new ASL contained no teams from New England, although there was an on-and-off (mostly off) New England Division for the next 20 years. The Metropolitan Division, as the main body was sometimes called, fluctuated a bit in membership, but its most frequent lineup in the first decades of the reborn ASL was two teams from the Bronx, two from Brooklyn, two from Kearny, two from Philadelphia and two from Baltimore. Occasionally, teams from Newark, Paterson or Trenton also were members.

IN THE FIRST SEASON of the renewed American Soccer League, the Kearny Scots had tradition, which the Kearny Irish did not. There had been no earlier Kearny Irish soccer team. The Kearny Irish had something as good as tradition, however. They had Archie Stark.

It should not be taken as surprising that a man who had been born in Scotland and lived there until he was almost a teenager opted to play for the Irish team rather than the Scottish one. Ethnically based American soccer teams in the middle of the 20th century often veered away from a strictly ethnic makeup. Examples of this among fairly prominent players have included John Wojciechowicz of Kearny Scots, Chico Chachurian of New York Swiss, Ed Murphy of Chicago Slovak and Jorge Benitez of Philadelphia Ukrainian Nationals and Los Angeles Yugoslavs.

In the 1933–34 ASL season, the first of the revived league, the players for one of the Kearny teams over the course of the season were McAteer, Parodi, O'Donnell, Patenaude, O'Brien, Harris, Black, Quick, Stark, Strong, McCartin, Mattade, Brown, Gavin, Blair, Kincaid, Clarke, Wisneski, McNally, Zbikowski, Kenny, Cahill, Mazza, Robinson, McTague, Touley, Sheppell and Aitken. The players for the other were Briscoe, McKay, Patterson, Walker, Sprague, Perry, Jogis, Kelly, Eaglesham, Carroll, Lennon, McGregor, Clark, Sheppell, Richmond, Brown, Davis, Conn, Johnson, Spied, Boyle, Davies, Christie, Malloy, Jamison, McLean, Adams, Nazzaro, Currie, Glenn, Ruddy, Douglas, McDonald, and Pierce. It doesn't appear obvious at a glance which was the Irish team and which was the Scottish team, does it? Not many of those names are immediately identifiable as Irish or Scottish, and some that are are on the "wrong" side of the equation.

WHETHER THEY WERE ALL IRISH—or Polish, Italian, Scottish or French—the Kearny Irish had a banner season in 1933–34. The Kearny Irish, for a while in the 1940s called Kearny Celtic, played for nearly 20 years in the ASL. They won their only league championship in the 1933–34 season.

Both Kearny Irish and Kearny Scots played in the 1933–34 season at Clark Field, where grandstands were filled to their 5,000 capacity for "derby" games between the two, of which there were several that season.

Kearny Irish won that 1933–34 ASL title on the strength of a long surge in mid-season that carried them clear of the opposition. In particular, it gave them a margin of safety against a late-season rush by the New York Americans, who ended up in second place.

For the first two months of the season, which began on Sept. 24, 1933, the Kearny Irish battled about evenly in the standings with the New York Americans and the Newark Germans. But between a 2–1 loss to the Brooklyn FC on Nov. 26, 1933 and a 5–0 loss to the New York Americans on May 27, 1934, they went 16 consecutive games without a defeat, winning 11 of those. Particularly crucial was a streak of four straight victories in February and March in which they widened their lead in the standings from five points to 11 and basically put the championship away.

Kearny Scots finished third that season, well behind both Kearny Irish and New York Americans, but they made a crucial contribution to the their local rivals' success. On March 18, 1934, as the New York Americans were seeking to close the gap that the Kearny Irish had opened, the Scots scored a 2–1 victory over the New York team, helping the Irish to tighten their grip on the championship.

There were two games between the Kearny Irish and the Kearny Scots during the last three months of that season, and both had a lot to do with the success of the Irish. The more critical of those games was played on March 4, and resulted in a 2–0 victory for the Irish that boosted them seven points ahead of the New York Americans. According to the *Newark Evening News*, the Irish played their best soccer in the first half in front of an overflow crowd at Clark Field, despite scoring both of their goals in the second half.

The newspaper reported:

"Over-anxiety of the Irish forwards helped the Scots to keep the winners scoreless in this [the first] half. The Blue backs used good judgment in crowding the Irish forwards as the condition of the field in front of the west goals [Clark Field ran east-west] was such that it was difficult to maneuver with the ball. The Scots didn't give the Irish much chance to time their shots, with the result that goalie [Joseph] McGregor was usually in position to stop the hurried Irish drives. The Blue halfback line did yeoman work in this period.

"The winners lost little time in taking the lead as the game resumed. A scrimmage in front of the Scottish goal gave [Archie] Stark an opportunity to boot through the opening tally after five minutes. The Scots rallied strongly after this goal and had the Irish on the run for the next twenty minutes. The Scottish fowards muffed numerous chances to score through careless shooting, while goalie [Joe] Quick pulled the game out of the fire frequently with timely saves. The Irish defense covered itself with glory under fire in this half. Sammie Harris was the spark plug in the Green defensive machine, and covered plenty of ground to break up numerous plays. Johnnie Brown and [Pete] Mattade also showed fine form in stopping the Scots.

"The second Irish score was the result of smart soccer on the part of Archie Stark. The veteran center dribbled past the backs by swerving to the left, drew the goalkeeper out of position, and then centered to [Rob] Clarke, who had nothing to do but boot the ball between the sticks. The Scots threw caution to the wind in the final minutes in a desperate attempt to score, but the Irish defense sucessfully withstood the pressure."[4]

That day was the most important for the Irish en route to the championship. By the time they met the Scots again on April 22, the Irish had the title virtually sewed up. Their 4–3 victory that day kept their lead at 10 points and closed the door on the New York Americans' hopes of overtaking them.

The Irish had to rally to that victory, after the Scots had taken a 3–1 lead on two penalty kicks early in the second half. Archie Stark made it 3–2 by putting in the rebound of his own shot and then "only a few minutes had elapsed when Stark knotted the count by outsmarting the Scottish backs and hooking a difficult shot into the corner of the net."[5] Ed McCartin scored the gamewinner for the Irish.

Archie Stark was 36, and this was his last full season, although he did return for a few games later, but he apparently hadn't lost his touch. The three goals that he scored against the Scots on March 4 and April 22 helped him to tie for the ASL goalscoring championship that season. He and Razzo Carroll of the Kearny Scots each collected 22 goals.

THE 1933–34 SEASON provided the Kearny Irish with their only American Soccer League championship, and they never came really close again. For most of the rest of their existence, which ended in 1951, they were middle-of-the-table sort of team, with a few exceptions. They reached the semifinals of the league playoffs in 1938, before being knocked out by St. Mary's Celtic of Brooklyn. They finished third in 1946, four points behind the winner. They were second in 1950, six points behind the winner, They were third in 1951, seven points back. Most of their remaining glory came in the Lewis

Cup, a postseason competition that had been held several times by the original ASL and was revived by the second ASL in 1940.

The American Soccer League was capable of devising some very arcane playoff systems. Of course, the league knew which side its bread was buttered on and that playoffs weren't it. Exhibitions against visiting foreign teams were where the league made some money. In 1949, when a playoff was needed to break a tie for the league championship, the playoff game was held as a secondary event, a prelim to a game between an ASL all-star team and the touring Belfast Celtic team. When the playoff game ended in a tie, the overtime was played two hours later, after the Belfast Celtic game, which was too valuable to the league to be tampered with.

Perhaps the strangest ASL playoffs were the ones used to determine league champions in the late 1930s, but the Lewis Cup format was not far behind. Eight teams qualified for the Lewis Cup playoffs. Theoretically, this was the top eight teams in the final regular-season standings, but in reality it was the top eight who wanted to play. This often meant that the Baltimore teams, tired of travel distances and travel expenses by this point of the season, opted out of the Lewis Cup, so the remaining teams all qualified. Under the most often used format, the eight were divided into two groups of four for schedule purposes, and teams from the same city, such as Kearny or Philadelphia, usually were placed in the same group. The standings, however, were not divided. There, all teams were lumped together, with standings from first place to eighth. A team played four group games, two against its local rival, and one each against the other two teams in its group. The eight-team, one-group standings were maintained, even though teams had played different sets of opponents. The first-place and second-place teams in the eight-team standings then played the final.

The Kearny Irish reached the final five times, but only won it once. They lost to Brookhattan of New York in 1942, Philadelphia Americans in 1943, Baltimore Americans in 1947 and Philadelphia Nationals in 1949. Their lone victory came in 1944, when they defeated the Brooklyn Wanderers, 7–4, in the two-leg, aggregate goals final.

The Irish were known as Kearny Celtic at that point. They had taken over the name Celtic in 1942, once there was no longer a Brooklyn team in the ASL using that name. (Brooklyn St. Mary's

Celtic had dropped out of the league after the 1941–42 season.) They had to come from behind to win that final. They had played a 2–2 tie with the Brooklyn Wanderers in the first leg on a neutral site, Starlight Park in the Bronx. In the second leg, on the Brooklyn team's home field, they fell behind, 2–0, by the middle of the first half. Al Sasso, whose brother Tom also was on the team, brought them back, with a goal just before halftime and another in the middle of the second half. The game went into overtime after the Kearny team missed a penalty.

"It was all Irish in the overtime," the *Newark Evening News* said. "The Kearny kickers started the first extra period with a forceful offensive and forged to the front in the first five minutes, with Frank Smith scoring on a pass from [John] Clark. The combination Smith to [Chappie] Sheppell paved the way for the second Irish score before the end of the first overtime period. In the last overtime session, Smith put the game on ice when he connected with a pass from Sheppell."[6]

Only one member of the 1934 champion team was still playing for the Irish that day. That was fullback Sam Harris. Also on the Irish team that season, although he didn't play that day, was Billy Stark, Archie's son.

In several ways, the Kearny Irish took a back seat to the Kearny Scots. The Scots (often referred to by the newspapers as the "Kilties"; the Irish were the "Harps" or the "Shamrocks"), had that connection, albeit a tenuous one, to the pre-1920 team. The Scots also lasted a few years longer in the ASL. For a number of years, both teams played at Scots Field, the Scots as landlord and the Irish as tenants. And, most importantly, the Scots had a few more on-the-field honors. In particular, they won the ASL championship in five consecutive years, 1937 to 1941, the only such streak in the ASL's 62-year history, and possibly the high point in the entire history of West Hudson soccer.

THERE HAVE BEEN many great West Hudson players over the years. The honor roll includes these names, none of who was a fabulous national star: Bobby Aitken, Fred Shields, Wally Peters, Frank Fisher, Alex Rae, John Wojciechowicz and George Conn. What those seven men did was to play for Kearny Scots in every one of those five consecutive ASL championship seasons. A number of others played on a few of those teams, some very prominently, but only these seven played on all five.

In the first three seasons of the Scots' reign, the champion was decided by a series of playoffs. Here is how the playoff system, which was the same in each of those seasons, worked. The league was divided into an American Division and a National Division. The first three teams in each division made the playoffs. The winners of the two divisions were given byes into the semifinals. In the first round of the playoffs, the two second-place teams played each other and the two third-place teams played each other. In the semifinals, the two first-place teams played each other and the two first-round winners played each other. In the final, the two semifinal winners played each other. In short, the fact of making the playoffs at all and the first-round byes given the two division winners were the only rewards for finishing higher in the regular season. Other than that, the "reward" for finishing higher was a tougher playoff opponent. The two division winners didn't get to play lesser teams in the playoffs; they got to play each other. The two second-place finishers didn't get to play third-place teams; they got to play each other. Adding to the playoff difficulties were frequent delays. Winners on one side of the bracket often had to cool their heels for weeks waiting for the other side of the bracket to catch up.

KEARNY SCOTS didn't get off to a perfect start en route to that string of championships. In the 1936–37 regular season they finished second in their division, with 24 points to the 26 collected by Brooklyn St. Mary's Celtic. That earned the Scots the right to face Canton of Baltimore, on the road at Bugle Field in Baltimore, to open the playoffs on May 9, 1937. A first-half goal by George Conn and two in the second half by Alec Rae sent the Scots home an impressive 3–1 winner. For the semifinals against the Paterson Caledonians, again a one-game decision, they got to stay home at Clark Field, and came through a 3–2 winner on an overtime goal by Frank Moniz in what, according to the *Newark Evening News,* was a "rough and tumble" game.

The Scots led by 1–0 at the half. According to the newspaper: "The game developed into a slam-bang affair in the second stanza and combination play was forgotten as the players hacked away at each other in reckless abandon. The period was marked by seven-

teen personal fouls [not all that shocking a number by today's stan-
dards]. [Lou] Marraccini equalized for the Callies after 10 minutes of
play after taking a cross from [Frank] DeVivo. Rae sent the Kearny
eleven ahead a little later when he followed through on a shot by
Moniz. Just before full time Thape tied the score for the Callies following a corner kick.

"Moniz crashed through the winning goal in the final period of
the overtime, following an exchange of passes in front of the Callie
goal."[7]

In the final, the Scots didn't have to face the team that had beat-
en them in the regular-season standings. St. Mary's Celtic was eliminated by Brooklyn Hispano in a two-games-plus-overtime semifinal, and thus the Scots played Hispano for the championship. The
final was a two-game series, and the Scots broke it open in the first
game, beating Hispano by 5–2 at Clark Field, on two goals by Conn,
two by Fisher and one by Rae. Today, forcing soccer teams to play
on consecutive days is considered a terrible thing, but years ago it
was routine. So the teams lined up again a day later on neutral
ground, Starlight Park in the Bronx. The Scots' three-goal lead was
too much for the Brooklyn team to overcome, although they gave it
a good try, briefly cutting the margin to one on early goals by Fabri
Salcedo and Aldo Gianotti. A goal by Rae just after halftime got the
Scots going again. After two goals by Fisher later in the half, the
game finished in a 3–3 tie and the Scots took the championship.

A YEAR LATER, the Scots had a slightly shorter playoff route, thanks to
a first-place finish in the regular season. They had 20 points in the
National Division, to 17 for Brooklyn St. Mary's Celtic. That got them
a pass into the semifinals, where they met the American Division
winner, the Philadelphia German-Americans, a formidable team that
had won the ASL title in 1935 and the U.S. Open Cup in 1936.

This semifinal, against a quality opponent, may have been the
best performance in the Scots' history. They won the two-game,
total-goals series by 12–6, taking a 4–2 victory in the first game in
Kearny and a 8–4 runaway in the return match in Philadelphia.

In the opening game at Clark Field, an early goal by Ray
Richards left the Scots briefly trailing, but Conn had them even by
halftime and they pulled away thereafter, with a goal by Rae and
Conn's second and third of the game. Then in the second game, on

the Philadelphia team's home field on April 17, 1938, they really dominated.

"Only during the first half," said the *Philadelphia Inquirer*, "were [the German-Americans] able to keep pace with the short-passing Scots. . . . In the second session, the Newark eleven asserted its marked superiority and left no doubt of the ultimate decision." After the Germans tied the score at 3–3 early in the second half, "the Scots displayed almost complete mastery over their rivals . . . raiding the enemy nets at will."[8] Stewart Aitken scored three goals for the Scots that day, while Rae had two and Fisher, John McManus and Fred Shields one apiece. Fred Shields was the same person as Fred Zbikowski of the 1934 Kearny Irish. He wasn't the only star of this Kearny Scots team with an Anglicized name. Wally Peters had been born Walter Pericciuoli.

This time, the Scots did play St. Mary's Celtic in the final. The Brooklyn team had eliminated the Kearny Irish in the other semifinal, the closest that Kearny's "other" team had come to the ASL title since its 1934 triumph. Once again the final was a two-game series played on consecutive days, and once again it was a triumph in the first game that carried the Scots to victory. On May 21, more than a month after their semifinal, the Scots beat the Celtics, 4–2, in Kearny, with Fisher scoring all four goals. The following day, they played a 2–2 tie in Brooklyn (goals by Bobby Aitken and Rae), to wrap up the championship.

IN 1939, the Scots had help from a controversial goal by Wally Peters in advancing to the final. Again they had won the National Division and gotten a bye through the first round of the playoffs into a semifinal meeting with the American Division winner, this time Brookhattan of New York. They had taken the first leg of their semifinal, 4–2, but were trailing, 1–0, early in the second half of the second leg, and thus had only a one-goal lead over Brookhattan. Tom Connell of the *Newark Evening News* described the controversy:

"Peters let loose a looping shot from 30 yards out that was cleared by goalie [Phil] Newman who was standing just a few inches inside the goal-line when the ball neared him. It was a tight decision and rested on the angle from which one viewed the play as to whether the ball was in or not [the referee ruled that it was].

"The Brookhattan players, however, protested vigorously and

walked off the field. After much discussion they decided to resume play. The spirit of the Brookhattan team was broken when play was resumed and although the Truckers held their own, they just didn't seem to have the finishing power they needed."[9]

The Scots met the Philadelphia German-Americans again in the final and scored what seemed a relatively routine victory over the team that was to win ASL championships (with an altered name, thanks to World War II) in 1942, '44, '47, '48 and '52. Alex Mentiply, Alex Rae and Red Ballantyne scored for the Kearny team in a 3–2 victory in the opening leg in Philadelphia. A day later, the score was 4–2, for a total margin of 7–4, after the Scots had rolled up a 3–0 lead in the first half. Ironically, the semifinals hadn't been played on such a tight schedule as the final. The two legs of the semifinal between the Scots and Brookhattan were two weeks apart.

THAT 1938–39 SEASON was the end of multiple divisions and playoffs in the ASL, at least for many decades. The next season, the league reverted to a single division, with the champion determined by the standings.

The Scots won the 1939–40 championship by charging undefeated through the final five months of the campaign. They hadn't gotten a bad start, but not the one they would have liked. On Oct. 22, 1939, after six games, they had only six points in the standings. Those six games included a forfeit loss, for using an ineligible player in a game they had won, and their only loss on the field all season, 2–0, to Passon of Philadelphia. As part of their fast finish, they avenged that defeat on Feb. 25, when Passon came to Kearny and the Scots scored an 8–2 runaway.

The Scots were undefeated in their final 11 games that season, and clinched the title on the next-to-last Sunday of the season, with a 2–1 victory on the road against Brooklyn Hispano. That gave them 25 points in the standings (they added two more with a win over the Kearny Irish a week later), and guaranteed that they couldn't be overtaken. Following that loss to Passon in October, they compiled a marvelous record. They won four in a row, played a 3–3 tie with St. Mary's Celtic, and then finished the season with six more wins in a row.

Kearny Scots had more points than any other team that season, but because not every team played the same number of games that season, the championship actually was settled on a percentage basis. Kearny Scots, with 27 points from 17 games, had a .794 percentage. Second-place Baltimore SC, with 23 points from 17 games, was .676, and Brookhattan, with 23 points from 19 games, was .605.

THE LAST OF THE FIVE VICTORIES was very definitely the closest. Again, percentage decided the championship in the 1940–41 season. The Scots finished with 34 points from 23 games, for a percentage of .739. The Philadelphia German-Americans had 32 points from 22 games, for .727. If the Scots had had one point less, in other words if just one of their victories had been a tie, their percentage would have been .717 and they would have finished second.

The race, of course, came down to the last weekend of the season, March 29 and 30, 1941, on which the German-Americans played two games and the Scots one. The Philadelphia team, which was to change its name to Philadelphia Americans on Dec. 8, 1941, had to win both games to have a chance, and did. That meant that the Scots had to win their game, and they did. Playing on their home field, they scored a 1–0 victory over Philadelphia Passon, a team the German-Americans had beaten by 6–0 the day before.

The *Newark Evening News* commented on the weekend's events, saying:

"Oddly enough, the Scots scored their lone goal in the first period when they were playing against a strong headwind. After 20 minutes of raiding the Passon goal, Billy Cooper crashed through a sizzling drive from close range, following an exchange of shots. The Passon defense stiffened as the period progressed and held the kiltie offense principally to pot shots from long range. . . .

"The Philadelphia German-Americans wound up their campaign at home in a blaze of glory by scoring two victories over the weekend. On Saturday they trounced the Phillies [Passon's nickname], 6–0. Yesterday they blanked the strong Brookhattan Truckers, 2–0, to carry the fight for first place right down to the finish line. The Germans made a brilliant showing during the second half of the league race to climb from fourth place to be a serious contender for top honors."[10]

Unlike the season before, when they had finished strongly, the Scots had won this championship largely on the strength of victories in mid-season. They really made their move in December and

January, when they played eight games and collected 14 of a possible 16 points. During those same two months, the Philadelphia German-Americans, who had been going head-and-head with the Scots, fell behind, getting only five points from six games and rendering their late rush not enough.

In a championship race as close as this one, any victory is a crucial one, but two do stand out. One came on the first day of the season, Sept. 15, 1940, when the Scots gave the visiting German-Americans a 6–2 beating. The other was on March 2, 1941, with the Scots looking over their shoulder at the German-Americans, who had beaten them by 2–1 in Philadelphia a week before. On that day, playing on the neutral-for-a-day ground of Scots Field, the Scots beat the Kearny Irish, 4–1, and kept their late-season slide from getting out of hand. The Scots' goals that day were scored by Bobby Aitken, Russ Brown, Frank Fisher and Alex Rae. Sixth months earlier, in that crushing victory over the German-Americans, Brown had scored four goals, while John Wojciechowicz and Matt Martin had the others.

The Scots didn't come close to adding a sixth championship. In the 1941–42 season, they finished sixth in the ASL standings. Their great powerhouse was breaking up. The most serious loss was Wojciechowicz, one of the relatively few ASL players to be killed in World War II (another of those few, Walt Patykula, last seen in a burning plane over Tokyo, had played for the German-Americans in both of their games against the Scots in the 1940–41 season).

THE SCOTS were to have one more significant victory. They won the Lewis Cup in 1948 (neither they nor the Kearny Irish ever fared well in the U.S. Open Cup). By the late 1940s, however, the forces that had promoted soccer so well in the West Hudson area were on the wane. In particular, by the 1950s, Kearny's two biggest employers of Scottish immigrants were gone.

The Clark Thread Company completed its move to Georgia in 1947. It had followed up its construction of a mill in Clarkdale in 1931 with other Georgia mills in Toccoa in 1937 and Pelham in 1943, and then three mills in 1947, in Acworth, Albany and Thomasville.[11] In announcing the final moves on May 22, 1947, company president John B. Clark cited the labor market and labor costs in New Jersey as the main reasons for the move, and noted that the Clark mills in

New Jersey were the only thread mills in an area that had become a center for electrical instrument manufacturing.[12]

The departure of Clark Thread had a heavy symbolic effect on the West Hudson region. The area's oldest Scottish-based employer and its oldest sponsor of soccer teams was gone. But in terms of actual numbers of jobs, the sale of the Kearny Federal Shipyard at about the same time had a much greater impact.

The Federal Shipyard, built as a part of the United States' World War I effort, fulfilled its original purpose, mainly building cargo ships. After the war, it languished. Between 1922 and 1938, it delivered only 46 ships to buyers, an average of fewer than three per year.[13] World War II turned things around. The Hackensack River is not deep enough or wide enough to handle big ships like battleships or aircraft carriers, so the Federal yard specialized in smaller vessels, especially destroyers. During World War II, it was the U.S. Navy's top contractor for destroyers, building about one-fourth of the Navy's "tin cans." Between October 1941 and March 1945, it delivered 68 destroyers to the Navy,[14] an average of one every 18 days. In the course of the war, it cut the time needed to build a destroyer from 18 months to five months. And most important for the West Hudson area, at its World War II peak, it employed a workforce of 32,000.[15] Many of those thousands had learned their trades at shipyards in Scotland, where the valley of the Clyde is one of the world's great centers of shipbuilding.

The yard continued production after the war, but at a dwindling rate, and on Dec. 31, 1948, it was sold by U.S. Steel to the Navy,[16] which held it in reserve for possible future needs that never came before selling the property for other use in 1963.

THE LOSS OF CLARK THREAD and the Federal Shipyard did not throw West Hudson into a desperate situation like that of Fall River and New Bedford when the cotton industry departed in the 1920s. However, it didn't help matters any at a time when the ASL could have used some help.

The Kearny Scots and Kearny Irish were among a number of ASL teams that dropped out of the league in the early 1950s. (One of those, the Philadelphia Nationals, at least went out on top, closing their doors after having won the 1953 ASL championship in their final season.) The Irish gave up the ghost in mid-season, selling their franchise and many of their players to Newark Portuguese, a formerly amateur team, in December 1951. Most of the same team that had played Philadelphia Americans on Sunday, Dec. 2 as Kearny Irish played Kearny Scots on Sunday, Dec. 9 as Newark Portuguese. Few, if any, if the players were actually either Irish or Portuguese. The Scots lasted less than two years longer. They no longer owned Scots Field, which had been located at the foot of the ridge in Kearny, near the edge of the marshes, and played the 1952–53 season at a field in Harrison. In the summer of 1953, the league's directors granted the Scots a year off in which to try to find a playing site closer to their fans in Kearny. They never found one and never returned to the ASL.

The Scots' departure from the ASL didn't surprise the *Newark Evening News'* Tom Connell, who had pondered the situation at the time of the Kearny Irish's leave-taking in 1951. Wrote Connell:

"Professional soccer, never exactly a flourishing sport in the last 15 years, started on a serious decline during the war years. Steadily decreasing patronage over the last five years or so has put the local clubs in the red financially to the point where the game is virtually fighting to survive. The Scots-Americans and Irish-Americans, with the limited means at their disposal, have waged a gallant fight to keep the game alive in West Hudson.

"However, their efforts have fallen far short of the necessary measures to retain the 'dyed in the wool' fans as well as 'sell' new adherents to the game. The Irish-Americans gave up the struggle last week, after several years of financial loss, and decided to abandon the game in favor of amateur sports. The Scots-Americans, also suffering financial losses each year, expect to continue. . . .

"The falling off of interest in New Jersey has been due to many reasons. The collapse of the amateur movement during the war, a scarcity of qualified players, lack of resourcefulness to meet changing conditions, insufficient funds for promotion and inadequate playing fields all have been part of the picture. The decline in interest is evident at the lower levels. Twenty years ago, West Hudson alone supported five leagues, in addition to having member clubs in the then strong New Jersey State League. Juvenile, junior and amateur players were active in a series of leagues under an arrangement whereby a player could advance through the ranks.

"But supporting two pro clubs in West Hudson gradually

drained off players and fans from the amateur clubs, with the result that a steady decline set in in amateur ball. This was hastened by the outbreak of World War II and one amateur league after another folded up. When the war ended, no concerted promotional effort was made to re-establish interest in amateur ball, with the exception of the German-American League, which attracted many of the better amateur players. With amateur ball falling off, the pros found qualified players were hard to find and there was not enough money to attract foreign players. Consequently, the caliber of play dropped considerably and with it the attendance."[17]

WHILE PROFESSIONAL SOCCER was having its turn on the stage in West Hudson during the 1930s and '40s, the amateur side of the game was coming to the fore in southeastern New England, after decades of professional or semipro Marksmen, Whalers and Rovers. With it, soccer played by Portuguese-speaking players became the best in the region, and might, for a few years, have been the best in the country.

For the most part, that strength came in the form of the Ponta Delgada club of Fall River, whose very name reflects the split in which Portuguese-speaking immigrants to New Bedford were predominantly from the western Azores and those to Fall River from the eastern Azores. The city of Ponta Delgada is the capital of the island of Sao Miguel, the largest island of the eastern Azores.

Ponta Delgada, like the Fall River Marksmen, actually played their home games in North Tiverton, R.I., although the field was no longer called Mark's Stadium. The Portuguese social club that spawned the Pontas still exists and is located right next to where the team played, beside the open field that is mentioned in the Introduction of this book.

WHEN PONTA DELGADA first won the National Amateur Cup in 1938, it wasn't obvious that this was the start of a new dynasty. It looked like just another very good amateur club from the Portuguese population of southeastern Massachusetts. The following year, St. Michael's of Fall River won the same title, and two years later Fall River Firestone narrowly lost in the final. But Ponta Delgada wasn't done. The club broke up during World War II but was restarted immediately after the war, principally thanks to the efforts of one of the players, Frank Moniz, who also had played for Kearny Scots in their glory years.[18] By the time it was done winning national titles, in the 1950s, it had won the National Amateur Cup six times, including a three-in-a-row run in 1946, '47 and '48. It had become the first team ever to win both the National Amateur Cup and the U.S. Open Cup in the same year, accomplishing that feat in 1947. It had represented the United States as the national team at the North American Championships in 1947. And it had supplied a large number of players to the United States' efforts in the 1948 Olympic Games in England, World Cup qualifying in 1949 and the 1950 World Cup in Brazil.

This was probably aided by a bit of an economic revival in Fall River. The city's finances, which had been taken over by the state of Massachusetts in 1931 after Fall River declared bankruptcy, were returned to local control in 1941. The United States' war effort didn't make as much economic difference to Fall River as it did to places with big defense employers like shipyards and aircraft plants, but it helped. And the vacant textile mills, at least some of them, were put to a new use as the garment industry moved into Fall River. With that employment, of course, came the irony of shirts and dresses being stitched together in Fall River out of cotton cloth that had been made elsewhere.

THE 1938 PONTA DELGADA TEAM, which beat Heidelberg from Western Pennsylvania, 2–0, in the National Amateur Cup final, was managed by Manuel Correla. By the Pontas' later glory years, the managing reins had been taken over by a different man, Manuel Travers.

Although 1947 is the famous year in which the Pontas achieved their Open Cup-Amateur Cup double, they almost did it the year before. In 1946, they won their second National Amateur Cup, with a 5–2 victory in the final over Castle Shannon, like Heidelberg from the then-soccer-rich area just south of Pittsburgh. In the U.S. Open Cup, in which they reached the final 16 for the first time, they went all the way to the final before losing to Chicago Vikings. En route to that final, the Pontas had beaten three American Soccer League teams, each in two-leg, aggregate-goals series. In the eighth-finals, they beat the New York Americans, 2–0 and 3–2. In the quarterfinals, the victim was Brooklyn Wanderers, 2–1 and 3–1. In the semfinals, the Ponta won the first leg, 4–2, from Philadelphia Americans, then lost the second, 3–2, for a 6–5 aggregate victory.

In the final, Ponta Delgada gave the Chicago team a close battle.

In the first leg, in North Tiverton, they played a 1–1 tie, with John Souza scoring the Pontas' goal. A week later, July 14, a 2–1 game at Comisky Park in Chicago gave the cup to the Vikings. Joey Chapiga scored for the Pontas. Vikings center forward Jimmy McDermott, playing his final game, scored both goals for his team.

IT HAS SOMETIMES been said that the Pontas were sent to play as the U.S. national team as a unit in the 1947 North American Championships because of the achievement of winning the Open Cup-Amateur Cup double, the first ever. Actually, this is not true. At the time of the trip to Havana, the Open Cup final against Chicago Sparta had not yet been played. The semifinals had, however, and the factors that sent the Pontas to the Caribbean probably included the fact that they had reached the final two years in a row, that they had won the amateur cup two years in a row and the impressive margin of their victory in the amateur cup final, 10–1 over Carondelets of St. Louis, a game in which Ed Souza scored five goals.

The Pontas had some eye-opening victories in the Open Cup as well. In the eighth-finals, they defeated Lusitano of Ludlow, Mass., another Portuguese team, 5–0. In the quarterfinals, it was 5–3 over the Philadelphia Americans, who were the ASL champions at the time, and which may have been most dramatic single victory the Pontas ever scored. The Philadelphia team appeared to have sewed up the victory when Bob Gormley's goal broke a 2–2 tie with just four minutes to play, but two minutes later, Ed Souza tied it again on a penalty. That sent the game into overtime, and goals by Souza and Frank Moniz gave the Pontas the victory. The semifinals against Brooklyn Hispano, a two-leg affair against another ASL team, produced an 11–1 aggregate score. The first leg, a 9–0 victory, was particularly remarkable because the Hispanos' goalkeeper, Gene Olaff, was one of the best in the country.

Because of the Pontas' trip to Cuba, the two-leg final wasn't played until Aug. 31 and Sept. 7, more than two months after the semifinals. Unlike the year before, the Pontas about wrapped things up in the first leg, at home, leaving little doubt about the outcome as they went to Chicago. The Pontas beat Sparta, 6–1, in that first leg, with Ed Souza scoring two goals, and John Souza, Ed Valentine, John Travis and Joe Ferreira getting one apiece. Despite going into the second game with a five-goal lead, the Pontas won that one anyway. Travis, Valentine and James Delgado scored the goals in a 3–2 victory at Sparta Stadium in Chicago.

The 14 Ponta Delgada players who played in the final, many of them in both legs, were Walt Romanowicz, John Machado, Manuel Martin, Joe Rego-Costa, Joe Ferreira, Joe Michaels, Jesse Braga (who was captain of the team), James Delgado, Frank Moniz, Vincent Luciano, Ed Souza, Ed Valentine, John Souza and John Travis.

Those same 14, plus Joe Machado, had made the trip to Cuba in July. That trip did not produce outstanding results. The United States/Ponta Delgada team finished last in the three-team competition. It lost to Mexico, 5–0, on July 13 and Cuba, 5–2, on July 20. Ed Souza and Ed Valentine scored the only Pontas goals. Perhaps the trip was most noteworthy for one name in the lineup. Joe Michaels didn't play the first game, but he did the second, thus making him the only man to play full international games for the United States both before and after World War II.

IN 1948, it was yet another Western Pennsylvania team that was the final victim as Ponta Delgada became the first team ever to win the National Amateur Cup three seasons in a row. Valentine, Travis, Chapiga and Bill Silvia scored the goals in a 4–1 win over Curry Vets on May 22, 1948. However, the Pontas came up short of making the U.S. Open Cup final for a third straight year. They beat Ludlow Lusitano again in the eighth-finals, 4–1, and the Elizabeth Sport Club of New Jersey, 2–0, in the quarterfinals. Their semifinal against Brookhattan of New York was a two-leg series, and the Pontas dropped both games, 2–1 and 2–0, to yield their title. However, by the time of those two games, on June 13 and June 20, the amateur Pontas had their eye on a competition that the professional Brookhattan did not, the Olympic Games.

Four Pontas players were members of the United States team at the 1948 Olympic Games in London. They were Ed Souza, Manuel Martin, Joe Rego-Costa and Joe Ferreira. Also on the squad was John Souza, who by then was playing for a different Fall River team, Lincoln. Martin was captain of the Olympic team, and was captain again when it played a full international against Norway en route home from the Olympics. All five Fall River players played in that game, and also did when the United States played Israel in New

York in September, a game that is not recognized by the USSF as having been a full international, but was the first game ever played by the fledging Israel, which had been a nation for only a few months. Rego-Costa was the United States captain in that game, and Ed Souza scored two of the American goals in a 3–1 victory.

1949 WAS NOT THE GREATEST of seasons for Ponta Delgada as a team. The Pontas failed to win a fourth consecutive National Amateur Cup, and while they met Ludlow Lusitano yet again in the eighth-finals of the U.S. Open Cup, this time the central Massachusetts team turned the tables on them with a 2–0 victory. Individually, however, they had some achievements. The United States qualified in 1949 to play its first World Cup in 16 years the next year in Brazil, and two Pontas players, John Souza and Manuel Martin, were a part of the qualifying effort. The qualifying series consisted of a three-team tournament in Mexico City in September 1949, with each team playing each of the others twice and the first two finishers qualifying for the World Cup. Souza and Martin played all of the United States' four games. Souza scored one of the goals that enabled the Americans to break the game open early in the 5–2 win over Cuba on Sept. 21 with which they clinched a World Cup berth. In additional to these games, Martin and Souza both played for the United States in a full international against Scotland in New York, as did Frank Moniz.

PONTA DELGADA nearly won the double again in 1950. It won the National Amateur Cup for a fifth time, beating Harmarville, another Pittsburgh area team, in the final. Harmarville won the first leg, 1–0, but Ponta Delgada took the second, 4–1, as Ed Souza scored a hat trick, to collect the cup. The Pontas again reached the final of the U.S. Open Cup, but lost to Simpkins of St. Louis, a team that featured several of the outstanding St. Louis players of that era. The Ponta Delgada team had several veterans of earlier triumphs, such as both Souzas, Joe Rego-Costa, Joe Ferreira, Jesse Braga and Frank Moniz. One of the new faces for the Pontas was Aldo Gianotti, a Fall River boy who had made a name playing for Brooklyn Hispano in the ASL a decade earlier.

The Pontas dropped the first leg of the final, 2–0, in St. Louis, and that made the difference. Two weeks later, they played a 1–1 tie with Simpkins in North Tiverton, getting a goal from Ed Souza, and were unable to regain the cup. In earlier rounds, Ponta Delgada had once again eliminated Ludlow Lusitano in the eighth-finals, and then polished off Brookhattan in the quarterfinals and Philadelphia Nationals in the semifinals.

Both Souzas were on the United States squad in that year's World Cup in Brazil, and both played in one of the most famous games in American soccer history, the 1–0 upset over England in Belo Horizonte. Among the many myths concerning American soccer is one, perhaps spawned that day by English writers, that the two Souzas were brothers. In truth, they were not related. The myth might never have gotten going if the people who started it had known how common Portuguese names like Souza were in Fall River. John Souza played all three of the United States games in that World Cup, against Spain, England and Chile. Ed Souza played only the last two. The United States team in the famous game against England included six players who had played in the U.S. Open Cup final two months before, the two Souzas from Ponta Delgada and Frank Borghi, Charlie Colombo, Gino Pariani and Frank Wallace from Simpkins.

PONTA DELGADA won one more National Amateur Cup when it beat Chicago Slovak, 2–0, in the 1953 final. Ed Souza, who scored both goals that day, was back with the Pontas after a spell with the German-Hungarian team of New York. John Souza also had moved to the German-Hungarians, where the two Souzas won the Open Cup-Amateur Cup double again in 1951, but he never returned to Fall River, having found employment in New York with the knitting mills that sponsored the German-Hungarian team. Both Souzas played for the United States against Scotland in 1952, when the Americans lost before a crowd of 107,765 in Glasgow. (There also was one Kearny player in that team, Dick Roberts of Kearny Scots.) Both Souzas were to play their final games for the United States against Mexico in 1954. John Souza was still with the German-Hungarians at that time, while Ed Souza was by then playing for Pawtucket Rangers.

PAWTUCKET HAD ITS SAY in the soccer of the 1940s also. Pawtucket Rangers, a continuation of the team that had earlier been called J&P

Coats, won the U.S. Open Cup in 1941 and were runnerup in 1942. The 1941 team beat Chrysler of Detroit in both legs of the final, winning by 4–2 in Pawtucket and 4–3 in Detroit. Appropriately, the last of those eight Pawtucket goals was scored by Tom Florie, then in the twilight of his career. A year later, the Pawtucket team appeared possibly headed for another title, after having eliminated Brooklyn Hispano in the quarterfinals and the ASL champion Philadelphia Americans in the semifinals. They came up short in the final, however. Gallatin of Pittsburgh won the first leg, 2–1, on its home ground, and then took a firm grip on the title with a 4–2 victory in Pawtucket.

BOTH PAWTUCKET RANGERS and Ponta Delgada were involved at one time or another in the New England Division of the American Soccer League, which had two incarnations and never did really get off the ground. The first incarnation stumbled along from 1933 to 1941 before folding, giving a good imitation of the sputtering Southern New England Soccer League of several decades before. The second incarnation gave it another unsuccessful try from 1951 to 1953.

Thus, at about the same time as big-time soccer in the West Hudson region of New Jersey breathed its last, or at least went into hibernation, big-time soccer in southeastern New England expired as well. In both places, there have been stirrings in the years since, but nothing like what went on before.

V

Since the Glory Years

T HE FORCES that brought soccer to West Hudson and southeastern New England in the 19th century were very similar. The
departure of those forces in the 20th century was similar, too.
By the 1960s, the textile industry was gone from both places, along
with the other factors that had brought large-scale immigration.
Soccer was not completely gone, but it certainly was not the big deal
that it once had been.

In Fall River, where the last textile mills finally closed in the
1960s,[1] the garment industry that occupied the mills after the departure of most of the textile industry in the 1920s is now itself gone,
much of it to the Third World. The labels inside American customers' shirts and dresses are much more likely to say that they
were made in Indonesia or the Dominican Republic than in
Massachusetts. Those mills, at least some of them, now are occupied
by factory outlet stores, and Fall River is hoping that attracting customers seeking inexpensive merchandise will help to revitalize it.

The center of Fall River has a different look, too. One thread of
the Interstate Highway System that was built all over the United
States in the 1950s and '60s bisected Fall River. Interstate 195, which
connects the Providence area with Cape Cod, cuts right through the
middle of the city, and much of the Quequechan River now is buried

out of sight, flowing through pipes beneath the new construction.[2] That construction also included a new city hall, dramatically straddling the highway, which passes through a tunnel underneath it.

In each of the three main soccer cities of southeastern New England, making use of its local history was a key part of its revitalization efforts in the latter part of the 20th century. In Pawtucket, which had not been as dependent on the textile industry as Fall River and New Bedford, and thus was not as hard hit by its departure, the original Slater Mill was the center of an historic district devoted to the beginnings of the American textile industry and the American Industrial Revolution. New Bedford's distant whaling past, far more glamorous than its more recent cotton past, was the center of efforts to attract tourism, efforts that even included a New Bedford Whaling National Park. And in Fall River, the "Lizzie Borden industry" celebrated Fall River's most famous character, who may or may not have murdered her parents one morning in 1892.

In Kearny, Clark Thread and the Federal Shipyard were gone by the late 1940s, but West Hudson had succeeded over the years in diversifying its industry, and was able to handle those departures relatively well. Other employers, such as DuPont Chemical, Western Electric and Ford Motor in Kearny, and Crucible Steel and Otis Elevator in Harrison helped to take up the slack. Thus, while West Hudson and southeastern Masschusetts certainly weren't the thriving places in the last quarter of the 20th century that they had been 100 years before, they weren't parts of the Rust Belt like many former factory towns elsewhere.

West Hudson has seen some changing immigration patterns. Signs in Spanish and Portuguese have become common in the windows of businesses along Kearny Avenue, including even the tavern that once was owned by Archie Stark. The land that once was Scots Field became the parking lot of the Hindu Community Center. For a while, the mayor was named Santos. (Unlike that in New England, the Portuguese-speaking immigration to Kearny has come primarily from Brazil.) The old Scottish flavor is not completely gone, however. Kearny still has a few Scottish restaurants and stores, and it still is one of the few places in America where renting a kilt is as easy as renting a tuxedo.

Immigration to Fall River has not changed much in decades. The flood of immigration from Lancashire and elsewhere in Britain stopped many decades ago, but Fall River's population still is predominantly white and its largest ethnic group still is Portuguese. In the Columbia Street area just south of downtown, Fall River's Portuguese heritage is very evident, as much so as the Scottish heritage in Kearny. The size of Fall River's population, about 90,000, is down some from the 130,000 peak of Fall River's boom years in the early 1900s.[3] In the meanwhile, Kearny has been slowly growing, and by the late 20th century had a population around 40,000.

IN BOTH KEARNY AND FALL RIVER, by the latter decades of the 20th century, some of the best soccer to be seen in America was not really very far away. For fans in Kearny, that meant Giants Stadium, part of the Meadowlands sports complex about six miles to the north. In Fall River, it meant Foxboro Stadium, about 25 miles distant.

Big-time soccer first came to Giants Stadium in 1977, when the New York Cosmos of the North American Soccer League moved there. That was the last of Pele's three seasons with the Cosmos and the first of Franz Beckenbauer's and Carlos Alberto's years with the New York team, and those players drew a lot of spectators, many of whom probably came from the West Hudson area. The Cosmos set a series of attendance records that season, topped by the 77,691 who saw them win a playoff game against Fort Lauderdale on Aug. 4, 1977. That was only the beginning, however. Through 2004, of the 59 American soccer crowds of 70,000 or more, 24 had been at Giants Stadium. The largest of those was 79,005, for an exhibition between Manchester United of England and Juventus of Italy in 2003.

Giants Stadium hosted games in the 1994 World Cup and the 1999 Women's World Cup, but was passed over for the 2003 Women's World Cup, supposedly because of controversy over wear and tear on the field between the stadium authorities and the National Football League teams who were its primary tenants.[4] This controversy over grass was a part of what prompted the desire by MLS' MetroStars to move out of the stadium where they had played since the league's inception in 1996. Their target was Harrison, one of the West Hudson towns. By the beginning of 2004, it appeared that the MetroStars' proposed Harrison stadium was going to be built, after several starts and stops, roadblocks and solutions along the financial and zoning trails, but many fans were taking a wary,

I'll-believe-it-when-I-see-it attitude. According to the MetroStars plans, however, it would not be on the same land where the great West Hudson teams of around 1910 had played. The location that the MetroStars were eyeing was a few blocks to the east.

DURING THE COSMOS' GREAT YEARS at Giants Stadium, there was one other connection between that team and West Hudson, perhaps a closer one than just the likelihood that many West Hudson residents were in the stands. One of the Cosmos' ballboys was a Kearny youngster named John Harkes, who was to become almost as famous as some of the players on the field at those games.

Harkes, who was born and raised in Kearny, but whose parents had been born in Scotland, became in the 1990s the most prominent soccer player produced by Kearny since people like Archie Stark and Davie Brown three-quarters of a century before. Midfielder Harkes played for youth teams in Kearny, for Kearny High School, for the University of Virginia, and then broke into the big time. He was one of the stars of the United States team at both the 1988 Olympic Games in South Korea and the 1990 World Cup in Italy. Following that World Cup, he went to work on attempting to gain a place in the British pro ranks, and eventually caught on with Sheffield Wednesday in the English second division. He was a major part of Sheffield Wednesday's efforts in the 1990–91 season, when it won promotion to the first division (the name used by the top rung of English soccer before the creation of the Premier League) and won the English League Cup. Harkes was the first American ever to play in a cup final at Wembley. This was only the League Cup, not the F.A. Cup, but the following season he and Sheffield Wednesday reached the finals of both tournaments. Harkes again played for the United States in the World Cup in 1994, and then returned to the United States at the start of the first MLS season in 1996, captaining D.C. United to the first two MLS championships. Harkes retired from playing professional soccer after the 2002 MLS season.

Harkes wasn't the only prominent player produced by Kearny in the 1990s, as that town regained a good measure of public recognization as the nation's leading "Soccertown." Tony Meola, a teammate of Harkes at Kearny High School and the University of Virginia, was the United States national team goalkeeper from 1989 to 1994. Tab Ramos, born in Uruguay, lived in Kearny and played for one of the nation's leading Catholic high school teams, St. Benedict's Prep in Newark. Ramos also was a mainstay of the United States national team in the 1990s, playing in the 1990, 1994 and 1998 World Cups. The dynamic Harkes and the skillful Ramos, both spectacular dribblers, were one of the greatest midfield tandems the United States has ever had.

FALL RIVER'S LAST HURRAH in professional soccer lasted a bit longer than Kearny's. Fall River SC played six seasons in the ASL in the late 1950s and early 1960s, but it gained its greatest success in the U.S. Open Cup. Fall River SC reached the latter stages of the U.S. Open Cup five seasons in a row, the final in 1959, the semifinals in 1960, the quarterfinals in 1961, the eighth-finals in 1962 and the quarterfinals in 1963. It very nearly became yet another Fall River team to take that championship in 1959, when it lost the final by 4–3 to the McIlwaine Canvasbacks of San Pedro, Calif. It also contributed one last Fall River player to the United States national team. That was Henry Noga, who was the goalkeeper when the United States played two World Cup qualifying games against Mexico in 1960. A bit more ASL success for southeastern New England came in 1974 when the Rhode Island Oceaneers, who played their home games in East Providence, R.I., won the league championship.

After that, there wasn't much in the way of big-time soccer in southeastern New England until 1991, except for the NASL's New England Tea Men in Foxboro and the occasional visits to Bigberry Stadium in Fall River of touring Portuguese pro teams. In 1991, however, the U.S. national team began playing regularly at Foxboro. In 1997, 2000, 2001 and 2004, the United States played a total of six World Cup qualifying games in Foxboro. The most crucial of those probably were a 2–2 tie with Mexico in 1997, surely something of a surprise to the visitors, and a 2–0 victory over Jamaica in 2001 that clinched the United States' place in the 2002 World Cup. Equally famous, however, was a 2–0 defeat of England a semi-exhibition in 1993, a stunning upset against a team that had won four in a row from the United States since the 1950 surprise in Belo Horizonte.

Foxboro hosted games in the 1994 World Cup, the 1999 Women's World Cup and the 2003 Women's World Cup, the first two at Foxboro Stadium and the third at the new Gillette Stadium after its predecessor had been demolished. In addition, the New

England Revolution of MLS were occupants of the two stadiums. In their first few seasons, the Revs were consistently a middle-of-the-standings sort of team, but regularly were one of the league's best drawing teams. In 2002, they rewarded those loyal fans by reaching the MLS championship game, which drew a crowd of 61,316 at Gillette Stadium.

As with Kearny and Giants Stadium, it is impossible to know how many of the fans at games in Foxboro were from Fall River, but some of them must have been. MLS paid a lot of attention to its Hispanic fans, and the Revs were very much aware of this factor, too, making special efforts to court the Portuguese community.

Still, while Fall River probably has a slight edge over Kearny in the matter of which has had a more glorious soccer history, there is very little evidence in Fall River today of its soccer past.

THE FACT THAT THE PROS were long gone from West Hudson and southeastern Massachusetts did not mean that those areas were completely immune to the amateur soccer boom that overtook the United States in the 1990s. Amateur soccer continued there, more so in Kearny than in Fall River. Still, there is a good soccer field less than a mile from the site of the Fall River East Ends Football Grounds, in Britland Park, where Bigberry Stadium once was located.

Despite dropping out of the American Soccer League, the Kearny Scots have continued down the years as an outstanding amateur club. In 1975, they reached the final of the National Amateur Cup and in 2003, they reached the semifinals, losing in overtime to the perennial powerhouse Milwaukee Bavarians. Youth teams, which play at several good fields in Kearny, particularly the Gunnell Oval, are the reason why Kearny has been able to produce excellent young players like Harkes, Ramos and Meola, who once were teammates with the Kearny Thistle youth team.

Kearny High School and Harrison High School both have had strong soccer teams over the years, frequently winning New Jersey state honors and other championships. The meetings between them are the closest thing there is in West Hudson these days to a local derby.

At the high school level in southeastern New England, there is a rivalry between New Bedford High School and Fall River's B.M.C. Durfee High School, but it does not compare with the rivalry between those two schools in basketball.

What it all adds up to is that soccer in those two areas still exists, but it is not what it was. Nor, considering what it was, should it be expected to be.

SOCCER IS DOING WELL in the United States early in the 21st century. The Major League Soccer men's league seems to be gaining the strength to survive, although the Women's United Soccer Association closed its doors in 2003. The United States men performed very well in the 2002 World Cup. The United States women have won the World Cup in 1991 and 1999 and the United States has successfully hosted excellent editions of the Women's World Cup in 1999 and 2003. American youth teams get stronger and stronger on the world stage.

Can the soccer events of the 1880s and 1920s and 1940s in West Hudson and southeastern New England be said to have been the cause of this? Unfortunately not. Maybe there is some thread there, but it is too tenuous to be a real cause-and-effect relationship.

Nevertheless, the events of the 1880s in West Hudson, southeastern New England and a few other places are the real, lasting beginnings of soccer in the United States, regardless of what did or did not happen in Boston in the 1860s. They may not have caused what is happening today, but they were a substantial part of the foundation on which today's structure was built.

In many parts of the world, particularly South America, the spread of soccer away from its British roots was a result largely of the leisure-time activities of British workers,[5] especially railroad builders. In the United States, it wasn't British railway workers, it was British textile workers. Possibly their effect would not have lasted for more than a few decades, however, were it not for another factor. There has long been a tendency by many immigrants in America, and children of immigrants, to try to Americanize themselves by taking up sports pursuits such as baseball and American football. But fortunately for the continued health of soccer in places like Fall River and Kearny, there were new immigrants, such as the Portuguese, Italians and "Syrians" in New England and new waves of Scottish immigration in Kearny, coming along behind the pioneers.

Soccer has had a difficult struggle in the United States. Sports is one of the ways in which Americans have sought to emphasize their differentness from other countries. Soccer was often labelled a "foreign sport" and pushed to the fringes of American sports consciousness. Fortunately, those fringes were real places, prominent among them Kearny and Fall River. The places that had nurtured American soccer in its earliest years helped to keep it alive as it grew but was threatened with being smothered by American sports. The arrival of the North American Soccer League and Pele in the 1970s sparked a soccer boom in the United States. Possibly that boom would have happened even if it had been necessary to build the sport from scratch in the United States in the last decades of the 20th century. Thanks to places like Kearny and Fall River, it wasn't necessary.

End Notes

INTRODUCTION

1. Roger Allaway, Colin Jose and David Litterer, *The Encyclopedia of American Soccer History.* (Lanham, Md.: Scarecrow Press, 2001). p. 5.
2. "The East End Club," *Fall River Herald,* April 25, 1891.
3. Clark Thread Company history, Rootsweb website www.rootsweb.com/~njhudson/enewark/ clark_thread_company_history.htm
4. James Waller, *The History of the Scottish Immigrant in Kearny, New Jersey, and Their Effect on the Culture of the Town.* (unpublished manuscript, 1973), p. 8.
5. T.M. Young, *The American Cotton Industry.* (New York: Charles Scribner's Sons, 1903), p. 3.
6. John T. Cumbler, *Working-Class Community in Industrial America: Work, Leisure and Struggle in Two Industrial Cities, 1880–1930.* (Westport, Conn.: Greenwood Press, 1979). p. 109.
7. Paul Gardner, *The Simplest Game: The Intelligent American's Guide to the World of Soccer.* (Boston: Little, Brown and Company, 1976). p. 36.
8. Bill Murray, *The World's Game: A History of Soccer.* (Chicago: University of Illinois Press, 1998). pp. 2–3.
9. Leo Pap, *The Portuguese-Americans.* (Boston: Twayne Publishers, 1981), p. 35.

10. Colin Jose, American Soccer League, 1921–31. (Lanham, Md.: Scarecrow Press, 1998). pp. 315–465.
11. Stephan Thernstrom, ed. *The Harvard Encyclopedia of American Ethnic Groups.* (Cambridge, Mass.: Harvard University Press, 1980). p. 910.

CHAPTER ONE

1. Daniel Van Winkle, *History of the Municipalities of Hudson County, New Jersey, 1630–1923.* (New York and Chicago: Lewis, 1924). p. 361.
2. E-mail from Roy W. Schlische, associate professor of structural geology, Rutgers University, May 27, 2003.
3. Van Winkle, p. 369.
4. Van Winkle, p. 362.
5. E-mail from Ken Forbes, East Newark history researcher, Jan. 28, 2001.
6. Philip T. Silvia, *The Spindle City: Labor, Politics and Religion in Fall River, Massachusetts, 1870–1905.* diss., Fordham University, 1973. p. 4.
7. Bill Reynolds, *Fall River Dreams.* (New York: St. Martin's Press, 1994). pp. 31–32, 34.
8. Henry Fenner, ed, *History of Fall River.* (Fall River: Fall River Merchants Association, 1911). p. 16.
9. Robert Grieve, *An Illustrated History of Pawtucket, Central Falls and Vicinity: Narrative of the Growth and Evolution of the Community.* (Pawtucket: Pawtucket Gazette and Chronicle, 1897). p. 126.
10. Susan Marie Boucher, *The History of Pawtucket, 1635–1976.* (Pawtucket: The Pawtucket Public Library and the Pawtucket Centennial Committee, 1986). p. 69.
11. John Williams Haley, *The Lower Blackstone River Valley: The Story of Pawtucket, Central Falls, Lincoln and Cumberland, Rhode Island.* (Pawtucket: Lower Blackstone District Committee of the Rhode Island and Providence Plantations Tercentenary Committee, 1936). pp. 58–59.
12. Local history, New Bedford Whaling Museum website http://www.whalingmuseum.org/city.htm.
13. Paul T. Rivard, *Samuel Slater: Father of American Manufactures.* (Pawtucket: Slater Mill Historic Site, 1974). p. 17.

14. Rivard, p. 19.
15. Rivard, p. 21.
16. Boucher, p. 61.
17. Rivard, pp. 27–28.
18. Caroline F. Ware, *The Early New England Cotton Manufacture: A Study in Industrial Beginnings.* (New York: Russell and Russell, 1931), p. 27.
19. Malcom Keir, *The Epic of Industry.* (New Haven: Yale University Press, 1926). p.149.
20. Ware, pp. 81–82.
21. Ware, p. 85.
22. Steve Dunwell, *The Run of the Mill: A Pictorial Narrative of the Expansion, Dominion, Decline and Enduring Impact of the New England Textile Industry.* (Boston: David R. Godine, 1978). p. 105.
23. Keir, p. 150.
24. Fenner, p. 17.
25. Keir, p. 148.
26. Dunwell, p. 104.
27. Dunwell, p. 104.
28. Dunwell, p. 106.
29. Philip T. Silvia, *Victorian Vistas; Fall River. Volume I.* (Fall River: R.E. Smith Printing, 1987), p. 4.
30. Silvia, *Victorian Vistas,* p. 7.
31. Maldwyn Jones, *Destination America.* (New York: Holt, Rinehart and Winston, 1976). pp. 107–108.
32. John Arlott, ed. *The Oxford Companion to World Sports and Games.* (London: Oxford University Press, 1975). p. 339.
33. Arlott, p. 80.
34. Richard Henshaw, *The World Encyclopedia of Soccer.* (Washington: New Republic Books, 1979). p. 465.
35. Arlott, p. 340.
36. John T. Cumbler, *Working-Class Community in Industrial America: Work, Leisure and Struggle in Two Industrial Cities, 1880–1930.* (Westport, Conn.: Greenwood Press, 1979). pp. 108–109.
37. Rowland Berthoff, *British Immigrants in Industrial America.* (New York: Russell and Russell, 1953). p. 12.
38. Jones, p. 107.
39. Cumbler, pp. 150–151.
40. James Kenyon, *Industrial Localization and Metropolitan Growth:*

The Paterson–Passaic Area. (Chicago: University of Chicago Press, 1960). p. 46.

41. Berthoff, pp. 41–42.
42. Dunwell, pp. 117–118.
43. Cumbler, pp. 114–117.
44. Jones, pp. 111–112.
45. T.M. Young, *The American Cotton Industry.* (New York: Charles Scribner's Sons, 1903), pp. 5–6.
46. Young, p. 20.
47. Berthoff, p. 35.
48. Mills history, Paisley on the Web website, www.paisley.org/paisley1/history/mills.php.
49. Coats Family history, Paisley on the Web website www.paisley.org/paisley1/history/coatsfamily.php.
50. Clark Thread Company history, Rootsweb website www.rootsweb.com/~njhudson/enewark/clark_thread_company_history.htm.
51. Gary Kulik, *Rhode Island: An Inventory of Historic Engineering and Industrial Sites.* (Washington: United States Department of the Interior, 1979), pp. 138–139.
52. Kulik, p. 139.
53. Van Winkle, pp. 370–371.
54. Berthoff, p. 44.
55. Stephan Thernstrom, ed., *The Harvard Encyclopedia of American Ethnic Groups.* (Cambridge, Mass.: Harvard University Press, 1980). p. 913.
56. Henshaw, p. 617.
57. Complete History of Nairn, Congoleum-Nairn website, www.nairnusa.com/DetailedHistory.html
58. Complete History of Nairn, Congoleum-Nairn website.
59. Complete History of Nairn, Congoleum-Nairn website.
60. James Waller, *The History of the Scottish Immigrant in Kearny, New Jersey, and Their Effect on the Culture of the Town.* (unpublished manuscript, 1973), p. 8.
61. Leo Pap, *The Portuguese-Americans.* (Boston: Twayne Publishers, 1981), pp. 18–23.
62. Seymour L. Wolfbein, *Decline of a Cotton Textile City: A Study of New Bedford.* (New York: Columbia University Press, 1944), p. 8.
63. Local history, New Bedford Whaling Museum website.

64. Daniel Georgianna, *The Strike of '28.* (New Bedford: Spinner Publications, 1993). p. 13.

65. Zephaniah Pease, *History of New Bedford.* (New York: Lewis Historical Publishing, 1918). p. 212.

66. Dunwell, p. 112.

67. Georgianna, p. 21.

68. Dunwell, p. 145.

69. Wolfbein, p. 73.

70. Dunwell, p. 107.

71. Young, p. 6.

72. Kier, p. 152.

73. Melvin Thomas Copeland, *The Cotton Manufacturing Industry of the United States.* (Cambridge, Mass.: Harvard University Press, 1912). p. 27.

CHAPTER TWO

1. Charles K. Murray, "History and Progress of the American Football Association," *Spalding's Official Association "Soccer" Foot Ball Guide, 1910–11.* (New York: American Sports Publishing Co., 1910), p. 27.

2. Murray, p. 27.

3. James Robinson, *The History of Soccer in the City of St. Louis.* (diss., St. Louis University, 1966), pp. 12–13.

4. Murray, p. 29.

5. "Canadians The Victors," *New York Times,* Nov. 29, 1885, p. 7.

6. "The Canadians Beaten," *Newark Evening News,* Nov. 26, 1886, p. 1.

7. "Football," *Toronto Mail,* Nov. 30, 1886.

8. "The East End Club," *Fall River Herald,* April 27, 1891.

9. "The East End Club," *Fall River Herald,* April 27, 1891.

10. "The Champions of America," *Fall River Herald,* April 16, 1888.

11. "Won By the Yankees," *Newark Evening News,* Feb. 23, 1887, p. 1.

12. "Won By the Yankees," *Newark Evening News,* Feb. 23, 1887, p. 1.

13. "Sketch of the American Association," *Fall River Herald,* April 27, 1891.

14. Colin Jose, *Keeping Score: Canadian Encyclopedia of Soccer.* (Vaughan, Ontario, The Soccer Hall of Fame and Museum, 1998), p. 44.

15. Jose, pp. 45–46.

16. Robinson, p. 24.
17. Robinson, p. 23.
18. Roger Allaway, Colin Jose and David Litterer, *The Encyclopedia of American Soccer History* (Lanham, Md.: Scarecrow Press, 2001), p. 29.
19. Allaway, p. 6.
20. Allaway, p. 180.
21. Lee I. Neidringhaus, "The Panic of 1983," Museum of American Financial History website http://www.financialhistory.org/fh/1998/61-1.htm
22. Neidringhaus.
23. Philip T. Silvia, *Victorian Vistas; Fall River. Volume II.* (Fall River: R.E. Smith Printing, 1987), p. 20.
24. Allaway, pp. 234–235.
25. Richard Henshaw, *The World Encyclopedia of Soccer.* (Washington: New Republic Books, 1979). pp. 151–152.
26. Murray, p. 31–32.
27. "National Association Foot Ball League of New Jersey," *Spalding's Official Association "Soccer" Foot Ball Guide, 1911–12.* (New York: American Sports Publishing Co., 1911), p. 107.
28. "West Hudson Soccer Football Club, Harrison, N.J.," *Spalding's Official Association "Soccer" Foot Ball Guide, 1911–12,* p. 129.
29. Allaway, p. 84.
30. "Newarks Lose to Rovers," *Newark Evening News,* Nov. 29, 1909, p. 19.
31. Steve Dunwell, *The Run of the Mill: A Pictorial Narrative of the Expansion, Dominion, Decline and Enduring Impact of the New England Textile Industry.* (Boston: David R. Godine, 1978). p. 112.
32. "Bethlehem Retains U.S. Soccer Title," *Bethlehem Globe,* May 8, 1916, p. 1.
33. Allaway, p. 15.
34. "Great Football Game," Fall River Herald, Sept. 14, 1906.
35. "Fall River Rovers Take Soccer Title," *New York Times,* May 6, 1917, section 3, p. 1.
36. "Bethlehem Steel Loses Championship," *Bethlehem Globe,* May 7, 1917, p. 8.
37. "Scots Beat Celts For American Cup," *Newark Evening News,* April 19, 1915, p. 22.

38. Charles K. Murray, "American Football Association Cup Competition, Season 1914–15," *Spalding's Official Assocation "Soccer" Foot Ball Guide, 1915–16.* (New York: American Sports Publishing Co., 1915), p. 36.

39. "Scots Beat Celts For American Cup," *Newark Evening News,* April 19, 1915, p. 22.

40. "Scots Victorious Over West Hudson," *Newark Evening News,* Feb. 22, 1915, p. 13.

41. "Scots Finalists in Cup Tie Play for U.S. Honors," *Newark Evening News,* March 15, 1915, p. 23.

42. C.H. Reynolds, "U.S.F.A. National Challenge Cup Final," *Spalding's Official Association "Soccer" Foot Ball Guide, 1918–19.* (New York: American Sports Publishing Co., 1918), p. 41.

CHAPTER THREE

1. William Robinson, "Fall River: A Dying Industry," *The New Republic,* June 4, 1924, p. 38.

2. Bill Reynolds, *Fall River Dreams.* (New York: St. Martin's Press, 1994), pp. 171.

3. Colin Jose, *American Soccer League, 1921–31.* (Lanham, Md.: Scarecrow Press, 1998), p. 10.

4. Leo Pap, *The Portuguese-Americans.* (Boston: Twayne Publishers, 1981), p. 35.

5. Pap, p. 20.

6. Stephan Thernstrom, ed., *The Harvard Encyclopedia of American Ethnic Groups.* (Cambridge, Mass.: Harvard University Press, 1980), p. 814.

7. Pap, p. 62.

8. Bill Reynolds, *Fall River Dreams.* (New York: St. Martin's Press, 1994), p. 172.

9. Jose, pp. 75–286.

10. "Report of the Honorary Secretary," *Spalding's Official Association "Soccer" Foot Ball Guide, 1922–23.* (New York: American Sports Publishing Co., 1922), p. 35.

11. Frank McGrath, "Sam Mark Brought Big-Time Soccer to FR Area," *Fall River Herald-News,* May 12, 1976.

12. Philip T. Silvia, *Victorian Vistas; Fall River. Volume III.* (Fall River: R.E. Smith Printing, 1987), p. 29.

13. John T. Cumbler, *Working-Class Community in Industrial America: Work, Leisure and Struggle in Two Industrial Cities, 1880–1930.* (Westport, Conn.: Greenwood Press, 1979), p. 138.

14. "Bethlehem Steel Loses Cup Classic," *Bethlehem Globe,* April 25, 1927, p. 8.

15. "Bethlehem Steel Loses Cup Classic," *Bethlehem Globe,* April 25, 1927, p. 8.

16. Philip T. Silvia, *The Spindle City: Labor, Politics and Religion in Fall River, Massachusetts., 1870–1905.* diss., Fordham University, 1973, p. 852.

17. Roger Allaway, Colin Jose and David Litterer, *The Encyclopedia of American Soccer History* (Lanham, Md.: Scarecrow Press, 2001), pp. 419–420.

18. "Fall River Soccer Team Transferred to New York City," *Fall River Herald News,* Feb. 16, 1931, p. 1.

19. Silvia, *Spindle City,* pp. 716–717.

20. Cumbler, p. 132.

21. Seymour L. Wolfbein, *Decline of a Cotton Textile City: A Study of New Bedford.* (New York: Columbia University Press, 1944), pp. 10–11.

22. Wolfbein, p. 11.

23. James Robinson, *The History of Soccer in the City of St. Louis.* (diss., St. Louis University, 1966), pp. 134–135.

24. Gary Kulik, *Rhode Island: An Inventory of Historic Engineering and Industrial Sites.* (Washington: United States Department of the Interior, 1979), p. 139.

25. Oscar Handlin, *A Pictorial History of Immigration.* (New York: Crown Publishers, 1972), p. 281.

26. Handlin, p. 284.

27. Stephan Thernstrom, ed., *The Harvard Encyclopedia of American Ethnic Groups.* (Cambridge, Mass.: Harvard University Press, 1980), p. 910.

28. Allaway, p. 274.

29. "One of Soccer's Greatest Warriors," *Fall River Herald-News,* July 23, 1977, p. 1.

30. Bob Broeg, "Gonsalves: 'No Equal' In American Soccer," *St. Louis Post-Dispatch,* June 15, 1973.

31. Steve Holroyd, "Billy Gonsalves: The Babe Ruth of American

Soccer," American Soccer History Archives website
www.sover.net/~spectrum/gonsalves.html

32. George Patzer, "Defenders Won National Amateur Cup 30 Years Ago; to Hold Reunion Next Saturday, *New Bedford Standard-Times,* June 1956.
33. Patzer.
34. Patzer.

CHAPTER FOUR

1. Edward Duffy, "Rebirth of the American Soccer League," *U.S. Annual Soccer Guide and Record.* (Brooklyn: William Graham, 1948), p. 63.
2. Letter from George Rogers, Kearny, N.J., April 2001.
3. Clark building choronology, Rootsweb website www.rootsweb.com/njhudson/enewark/ clark_building_erection_chronology.htm
4. Tom Connell, "Irish-Americans Smash Way to Soccer Lead in Victory Over Scots," *Newark Evening News,* March 5, 1934. p. 28.
5. Tom Connell, "Irish Booters Win as Scots Fail in Rally," *Newark Evening News,* April 23, 1934, p. 28.
6. "Irish Run Wild In Overtime Tilt," *Newark Evening News,* June 12, 1944, p. 20.
7. Tom Connell, "Scots Defeat Callies, Gain Playoff Final," *Newark Evening News,* May 17, 1937, p. 29.
8. Edward J. Klein, "Scots-Americans Easily Defeat German Soccermen," *Philadelphia Inquirer,* April 18, 1938, p. 18.
9. Tom Connell, "Scots Reach Soccer Final," *Newark Evening News,* May 29, 1939, p. 22.
10. Tom Connell, "Scots Tack on No. 5," *Newark Evening News,* March 31, 1941, p. 22.
11. Clark building choronology, Rootsweb website www.rootsweb.com/njhudson/enewark/ clark_building_erection_chronology.htm
12. "Old Newark Plant Moving to South," *New York Times,* May 24, 1947, p. 21.
13. Federal Shipbuilding Pre-WWII record, Colton Company

website www.coltoncompany.com/shilbldg/ussbldrs/
prewwii/federal.html

14. Federal Shipbuilding WWII record, Colton Company website
www.coltoncompany.com/shilbldg/ussbldrs/wwii/mer-
chantshipbuilders/federalkearny.html

15. James P. Johnson, *New Jersey, History of Ingenuity and Industry*.
Northridge, Calif.: Windsor Publications, 1987, p. 328.

16. "Navy Takes Over Kearny Shipyard," New York Times, Jan. 1,
1949, p. 27.

17. Tom Connell, "Pro Soccer Needs Shot in the Arm," *Newark
Evening News*, Dec. 9, 1951, section 4, p. 21.

18. Jim Donaldson, "In Fall River, title memories may never die,"
Providence Journal-Bulletin, July 25, 1981, p. B-6.

CHAPTER FIVE

1. Philip T. Silvia, *The Spindle City: Labor, Politics and Religion in Fall
River, Massachusetts., 1870–1905*. diss., Fordham University, 1973.
p. 717.

2. Fall River Open Space Plan, Green Futures website
www.greenfutures.org/projects/osp/section4c1.html

3. Fall River profile, Massachusetts Department of Housing and
Community Development website www.state.ma.us/dhcd/
profile/095.htm

4. Mike Jensen, "Philly nets Women's World Cup games," *Philadelphia Inquirer*, June 13, 2003, p. D1.

5. John Arlott, ed., *The Oxford Companion to World Sports and Games*.
(London: Oxford University Press, 1975). p. 344.

Glossary

This section is intended as a ready reference to help the reader keep straight the many leagues, teams and players mentioned in this book, particularly teams from the same city in different eras but with similar names, plus a few other soccer terms.

Aggregate score. The result of a series, usually a playoff, in which the teams play two games, home-and-home, with total goals in the two games determining the winner.

American Football Association. The first attempt to create a nationwide governing body of soccer in the United States, founded in New Jersey in 1884.

AFA Cup. The original championship of American soccer, a cup competition conducted by the American Football Association beginning in 1885.

American League of Professional Football Clubs. A short-lived league that lasted only three weeks in the fall of 1894, but which was the first professional soccer league in the United States.

American Soccer League I. The first truly first-division soccer league in the United States, founded in 1921 in the New England and Middle Atlantic states and lasting until the early 1930s.

American Soccer League II. The scaled back version of the ASL, intended to be more financially prudent than the first, which began play in 1933 and lasted until 1983. Only in its last 10 years or so did it expand beyond the East Coast.

American Soccer League, New England Division. A separate arm of the second ASL, in addition to its Metropolitan Division in the New York-Philadelphia-Baltimore area, but one that played only sporadically before dying out in the 1950s.

Bethlehem Steel. Team from the steel mills of Bethlehem, Pa., that was a perennial rival of Fall River teams for major honors from 1915 to 1930.

Brown, Davie. A lifelong Kearny resident who was second only to Archie Stark among the original ASL's greatest goalscorers.

Clark AA. The name used around 1910 by the Kearny team sponsored by the Clark Thread Mill that had earlier gone by the name ONT.

Double. Victories in both the national league championship and the national cup championship in the same year. In the United States, it has sometimes been difficult to determine what was the leading league.

Douglas, Jimmy. A Kearny native who played for the Newark Skeeters in the original ASL and was the goalkeeper for the U.S. World Cup team in 1930.

Fall River East Ends. The first Fall River soccer team, founded in 1880 near County Street and winner of the AFA Cup in 1891.

Fall River Marksmen. The great Fall River team of the original ASL, winning that league in 1924, '25, '26, '29 and '30 and the U.S. Open Cup in 1924, '27, '30 and '31.

Fall River Ponta Delgada. A Portuguese-based amateur team that floruished in the 1940s, winning the National Amateur Cup in 1946, '47 and '48 and the U.S. Open Cup in 1947.

Fall River Rovers. The main Fall River powerhouse of the early decades of American soccer, winning the AFA Cup in 1888 and '89 and the U.S. Open Cup in 1917 among other honors.

FIFA. The world govering organization of soccer, whose full French name is the *Federation International de Football Association.* It was founded in 1904 in Paris and now is located in Switzerland.

Florie, Tom. A New Jersey/New England hybrid, a forward who was born and raised in Harrison but had his greatest profession-al years in Providence and New Bedford. He played for the United States in the 1930 and 1934 World Cups.

German-American Soccer League. The leading amateur league in the New York area, which was founded in 1923 and is still play-ing today, although its name has been changed to the Cosmopolitan League.

Gonsalves, Billy. Inside forward who was the most famous player ever produced by Fall River, although he spent most of his play-ing career, from the 1920s to the 1940s, elsewhere.

Harkes, John. A midfielder from Kearny who was one of the great American stars of the 1990s, playing in two World Cups and for several seasons in England and Major League Soccer.

Harrison FC. A West Hudson team that played in both the NAFBL and the original ASL, under the name Erie AA in the former and Harrison FC in the latter.

J&P Coats. The leading Pawtucket team over the first three decades of the 20th century, sponsored by a Pawtucket thread-making company and playing in the Southern New England league and the orginal ASL.

Kearny Irish. The "other" Kearny team of the 1930 and '40s, play-ing second fiddle to Kearny Scots, but winning an ASL title in 1934.

Kearny Scots. A famous Kearny team that has had two incarna-tions, 1895 to 1919 and 1931 to the present, and which won five consecutive ASL titles in the 1930s and '40s. Possibly the oldest still operating soccer team in the United States.

Major League Soccer. Yet another attempt to start a professional soccer league in the United States, this one beginning in 1996 and seeming to have a possibility of success.

McNab, Alex. A Scottish-born winger who starred over the years in teams in Boston, Fall River, New Bedford and St. Louis and won a number of major championships.

McPherson, Bill. Another Scottish-born foward who starred for a series of teams in New England and St. Louis and won a string of major titles.

Meola, Tony. A goalkeeper from Kearny who played for the United States in the 1990 and 1994 World Cups and for a number of years in Major League Soccer.

MetroStars. A Major League Soccer team, originally called the New York/New Jersey MetroStars, that played at Giants Stadium while making plans to built a soccer-only stadium in Harrison.

Moniz, Frank. One of the few players who starred for teams in both Kearny and Fall River, for the Kearny Scots dynasty in the early 1940s and for Ponta Delgada later in that decade.

National Amateur Cup. A competition started by the USFA in 1923 to give a national championship outlet to amateur teams, who were being dominated by the pros in the U.S. Open Cup.

National Association Foot Ball League. The first really lasting soccer league in the United States. The NAFBL, centered in New Jersey, New York and Pennsylvania, played from 1895 to 1921.

National Challenge Cup. See U.S. Open Cup.

New Bedford Defenders. The first team from southeastern New England to win the National Amateur Cup, taking that trophy in 1926.

New Bedford Whalers. The most common name of athletic teams from New Bedford, most famously used by American Soccer League teams in the 1920s and '30s.

New England Revolution. A Major League Soccer team that played its games in Foxboro, Mass., about 25 miles north of Fall River.

New York Cosmos. The most famous team of the North American Soccer League, which played from 1977 to 1984 at Giants Stadium, six miles from Kearny.

New York Yankees. The name under which the Fall River Marksmen played briefly after moving from Fall River to New York City in 1931.

Newark Skeeters. One of the few New Jersey teams in the original ASL, which regularly finished well down in the standings.

Nilsen, Werner. One of the stars of the Fall River Marksmen powerhouse in the late 1920s and early 1930s, and a member of the 1934 United States World Cup team.

North American Soccer League. A big-time league, attracting a number of world stars, that lasted from 1968 to 1984 and had its peak, with crowds of over 70,000, in the late 1970s.

Oliver, Arnie. A leader of the New Bedford Defenders team that won the National Amateur Cup in 1926 and a member of the United States team at the 1930 World Cup.

ONT. The original team sponsored by Clark Thread Mills in the 1880s, and winner of the first three three AFA Cup championships.

Patenaude, Bert. The outstanding Fall River player of French-Canadian descent. A star of outstanding pro teams in the late 1920s and throughout the 1930s, and the scorer of the first hat trick in World Cup history.

Paterson True Blues. One of the strongest New Jersey teams, both before and after the hiatus of 1899–1905. Winner of AFA Cup titles in 1896, 1909 and 1913.

Pawtucket Free Wanderers. The first Pawtucket team to win a major championship, taking the AFA Cup title in 1893.

Pawtucket Rangers. The name used by what had been the J&P Coats team after the company's involvement ended. U.S. Open Cup winner in 1941, and runnerup in 1935 and '42.

Ramos, Tab. A midfielder who grew up in Kearny after having been born in Uruguay and played for the United States in the 1990, 1994 and 1998 World Cups as well as for pro teams in the United States and Spain.

Southern New England Soccer League. A struggling league, with some on seasons and some off, during the 15 years that preceded the start of the first ASL in 1921.

Souza, Ed. Forward from Fall River who played for the United States against England in the 1950 World Cup. Winner of the U.S. Open Cup in 1947 with Ponta Delgada and 1951 with New York German-Hungarian.

Souza, John. Forward from Fall River who was not related to Ed Souza but played for most of the same teams, including the United States in the 1950 World Cup, and was known by the nickname "Clarkie."

Stark, Archie. Scottish-born forward who lived in Kearny for most of his life. He played for clubs that included Kearny Scots, Bethlehem Steel and Kearny Irish, and became the greatest first-division goalscorer in American soccer history.

Swords, Thomas. The captain of both the Fall River Rovers team that upset Bethlehem Steel in the 1917 U.S. Open Cup final and the U.S. national team on its 1916 Scandinavian tour.

U.S. Football Association. See U.S. Soccer Federation.

U.S. Open Cup. The single-elimination tournament for the championship of the U.S. Soccer Federation, first held in 1914, which was called the National Challenge Cup in its early years.

U.S. Soccer Football Association. See U.S. Soccer Federation.

U.S. Soccer Federation. The governing organization of the sport in the United States, which was founded in 1913 as the U.S. Football Association and whose name was changed to U.S. Soccer Football Association in 1945 and to the current name in 1974.

West Hudson AA. Harrison team that was the best in New Jersey in the years just before World War I, winning the AFA Cup in 1906, '08 and '12.

White, 'Tec'. Forward who was one of the leading stars of the Fall River Marksmen powerhouse of the late 1920s and early 1930s.

Bibliography

BOOKS

Allaway, Roger, Colin Jose and David Litterer. *The Encyclopedia of American Soccer History*. Lanham, Md.: Scarecrow Press, 2001.

Arlott, John, ed. *The Oxford Companion to World Sports and Games*. London: Oxford University Press, 1975.

Bagnall, William. *The Textile Industries of the United States*. Cambridge, Mass.: The Riverside Press, 1893.

Berthoff, Rowland. *British Immigrants in Industrial America*. New York: Russell and Russell, 1953.

Boucher, Susan Marie. *The History of Pawtucket, 1635–1976*. Pawtucket, R.I.: The Pawtucket Public Library and the Pawtucket Centennial Committee, 1986.

Copeland, Melvin Thomas. *The Cotton Manufacturing Industry of the United States*. Cambridge, Mass.: Harvard University Press, 1912.

Cumbler, John T. *Working Class Community in Industrial America: Work, Leisure and Struggle in Two Industrial Cities, 1880–1930*. Westport, Conn.: Greenwood Press, 1979.

Dunwell, Steve. *The Run of the Mill: A Pictorial Narrative of the Expansion, Dominion, Decline and Enduring Impact of the New England Textile Industry*. Boston: David R. Godine, 1978.

Fenner, Henry, ed. *History of Fall River*. Fall River, Mass.: Fall River Merchants Association, 1911.

Gardner, Paul. *The Simplest Game: The Intelligent American's Guide to the World of Soccer*. Boston: Little, Brown and Company, 1976.

Georgianna, Daniel with Roberta Hazen Aaronson. *The Strike of '28*. New Bedford, Mass.: Spinner Publications, 1993.

Grieve, Robert. *An Illustrated History of Pawtucket, Central Falls and Vicinity: Narrative of the Growth and Evolution of the Community*. Pawtucket, R.I.: Pawtucket Gazette and Chronicle, 1897.

Groner, Alex. *The American Heritage History of American Business & Industry*. New York: American Heritage Publishing Co., 1972.

Haley, John Williams. *The Lower Blackstone River Valley: The Story of Pawtucket, Central Falls, Lincoln and Cumberland, Rhode Island*. Pawtucket, R.I.: Lower Blackstone District Committee of the Rhode Island and Providence Plantations Tercentenary Committee, 1936.

Handlin, Oscar. *A Pictorial History of Immigration*. New York: Crown Publishers, 1972.

Henshaw, Richard. *The Encyclopedia of World Soccer*. Washington: New Republic Books, 1979.

Johnson, James P. *New Jersey, History of Ingenuity and Industry*. Northridge, Calif.: Windsor Publications, 1987.

Jones, Maldwyn. *Destination America*. New York: Holt, Rinehart and Winston, 1976.

Jose, Colin. *American Soccer League, 1921–31*. Lanham, Md.: Scarecrow Press, 1998.

Jose, Colin. *Keeping Score: Canadian Encyclopedia of Soccer*. Vaughan, Ontario, The Soccer Hall of Fame and Museum, 1998.

Keir, Malcolm. *The Epic of Industry*. New Haven, Conn.: Yale University Press, 1926.

Kenyon, James. Industrial Localization and Metropolitan Growth: *The Paterson–Passaic Area*. Chicago, University of Chicago Press, 1960.

Murray, Bill. *The World's Game: A History of Soccer*. Chicago: University of Illinois Press, 1998.

Pap, Leo. *The Portuguese-Americans (The Immigrant Heritage of America Series)*. Boston: Twayne Publishers, 1981.

Pease, Zephaniah Walter. *History of New Bedford*. New York: Lewis Historical Publishing, 1918.

Reynolds, Bill. *Fall River Dreams*. New York: St. Martin's Press, 1994

Rivard, Paul T. *Samuel Slater: Father of American Manufactures*. Pawtucket, R.I.: Slater Mill Historic Site, 1974.

Shaw, William. *History of Essex and Hudson Counties, New Jersey*. Philadelphia: Everts and Peck, 1884.

Silvia, Philip T. *Victorian Vistas: Fall River*. Fall River, Mass.: R.E. Smith Printing, 1987.

Thernstrom, Stephan, ed. *The Harvard Encyclopedia of American Ethnic Groups*. Cambridge, Mass.: Harvard University Press, 1980.

Van Winkle, Daniel. *History of the Municipalities of Hudson County, New Jersey, 1630–1923*. New York, Lewis Historical Publishing Co., 1924.

Ware, Caroline F. *The Early New England Cotton Manufacture: A Study in Industrial Beginnings*. New York: Russell and Russell, 1931.

Wolfbein, Seymour L. *Decline of a Cotton Textile City: A Study of New Bedford*. New York: Columbia University Press, 1944.

Young, T.M. *The American Cotton Industry*. New York: Charles Scribner's Sons, 1903.

NEWSPAPER ARTICLES

Broeg, Bob. "Gonsalves: 'No Equal' In American Soccer," *St. Louis Post-Dispatch*, June 15, 1973.

Connell, Tom. "Irish-Americans Smash Way to Soccer Lead," *Newark Evening News*, March 5, 1934.

Connell, Tom. "Irish Booters Win as Scots Fail in Rally," *Newark Evening News*, April 23, 1934.

Connell, Tom. "Scots Defeat Callies, Gain Playoff Final," *Newark Evening News*, May 17, 1937.

Connell, Tom. "Scots Reach Soccer Final," *Newark Evening News*, May 29, 1939.

Connell, Tom. "Scots Tack on No. 5," *Newark Evening News*, March 31, 1941.

Connell, Tom. "Pro Soccer Needs Shot in the Arm," *Newark Evening News*, Dec. 9, 1951.

Jensen, Mike. "Philly nets Women's World Cup games," *Philadelphia Inquirer*, June 13, 2003.

Klein, Edward J. "Scots-Americans Easily Defeat German Soccer-men," *Philadelphia Inquirer*, April 18, 1938.

McGrath, Frank. "Sam Mark Brought Big-Time Soccer to FR Area," *Fall River Herald News*, May 12, 1976.

Patzer, George. "Defenders Won National Amateur Cup 30 Years Ago; to Hold Reunion Next Saturday," *New Bedford Standard-Times*, June 1956.

"Bethlehem Retains U.S. Soccer Title," *Bethlehem Globe*, May 8, 1916.

"Bethlehem Steel Loses Championship," *Bethlehem Globe*, May 7, 1917.

"Bethlehem Steel Loses Cup Classic," *Bethlehem Globe*, April 25, 1927.

"Canadians The Victors," *New York Times*, Nov. 29, 1885.

"Fall River Soccer Team Transferred to New York City," *Fall River Herald News*, Feb. 16, 1931.

"Fall River Rovers Take Soccer Title," *New York Times*, May 6, 1917.

"Football," *Toronto Mail*, Nov. 30, 1886.

"Great Football Game," *Fall River Herald*, Sept. 14, 1906.

"Irish Run Wild In Overtime Tilt," *Newark Evening News*, June 12, 1944.

"Navy Takes Over Kearny Shipyard," *New York Times*, Jan. 1, 1949.

"Newarks Lose to Rovers," *Newark Evening News*, Nov. 29, 1909.

"Old Newark Plant Moving to South," *New York Times*, May 23, 1947.

"Scots Beat Celts For American Cup," *Newark Evening News*, April 19, 1915.

"Scots Finalists in Cup Tie Play for U.S. Honors," *Newark Evening News*, March 15, 1915.

"Scots Victorious Over West Hudson," *Newark Evening News*, Feb. 22, 1915.

"Sketch of the American Association," *Fall River Herald*, April 27, 1891.

"The Canadians Beaten," *Newark Evening News*, Nov. 26, 1886.

"The Champions of America," *Fall River Herald*, April 16, 1888.

"The East End Club," *Fall River Herald*, April 25, 1891.

"Won By the Yankees," *Newark Evening News*, Feb. 23, 1887.

ARTICLES IN PERIODICALS

Cahill, Thomas W. "Report of the Honorary Secretary," *Spalding's Official Association "Soccer" Foot Ball Guide, 1922–23.*

Duffy, Edward. "Rebirth of the American Soccer League," *U.S. Annual Soccer Guide and Record, 1948.*

Murray, Charles K. "History and Progress of the American Football Association," *Spalding's Official Association "Soccer" Foot Ball Guide, 1910–11.*

Murray, Charles K. "American Football Association Cup Competition, Season 1914–15," *Spalding's Official Assocation "Soccer" Foot Ball Guide, 1915–16.*

Reynolds, C.H. "U.S.F.A. National Challenge Cup Final," *Spalding's Official Association "Soccer" Foot Ball Guide, 1918–19.*

Robinson, William. "Fall River, Mass.: A Dying Industry," *The New Republic,* June 4, 1924.

"National Association Foot Ball League of New Jersey," *Spalding's Official Association "Soccer" Foot Ball Guide, 1911–12.*

"West Hudson Soccer Football Club, Harrison, N.J.," *Spalding's Official Association "Soccer" Foot Ball Guide, 1911–12.*

UNPUBLISHED MATERIAL

Robinson, James. *The History of Soccer in the City of St. Louis.* Ph.D. dissertation, St. Louis University, 1966.

Silvia, Philip T. *The Spindle City: Labor, Politics and Religion in Fall River, Massachusetts, 1870–1905.* Ph.D. dissertation, Fordham University, 1973.

Waller, James. *The History of the Scottish Immigrant in Kearny, New Jersey, and Their Effect on the Culture of the Town.* 1973.

INTERNET WEBSITES

Billy Gonsalves, American Soccer History Archives website
www.sover.net/~spectrum

Coats Family history, Paisley on the Web website
http://www.paisley.org.

Complete History of Nairn, Congoleum-Nairn Company website
http://www.nairnusa.com.

Clark building chronology, Rootsweb website
http://www.rootsweb.com.

Clark Thread Company history, Rootsweb website
http://www.rootsweb.com.

Fall River Open Space Plan, Green Futures website
     www.greenfutures.org.
Fall River profile, Massachusetts Department of Housing and
     Community Development website www.state.ma.us/dhcd/.
Federal Shipbuilding WWII record, Colton Company website
     www.coltoncompany.com.
Federal Shipbuilding Pre-WWII record, Colton Company website
     www.coltoncompany.com.
Local history, New Bedford Whaling Museum website
     http://www.whalingmuseum.org.
Mills history, Paisley on the Web website http://www.paisley.org.
The Panic of 1893, Museum of American Financial History website
     http://www.financialhistory.org.

GOVERNMENT PUBLICATIONS

Kulik, Gary. *Rhode Island: An Inventory of Historic Engineering and
     Industrial Sites.* Washington: United States Department of the
     Interior, 1979.

Index